Once upon a time

Once upon a time

reflections on childhood

with a foreword by
MICHAEL ASPEL

collected by
Vince Powell
and **Greg Watts**

NSPCC
Cruelty to children must stop. **FULL STOP.**

continuum

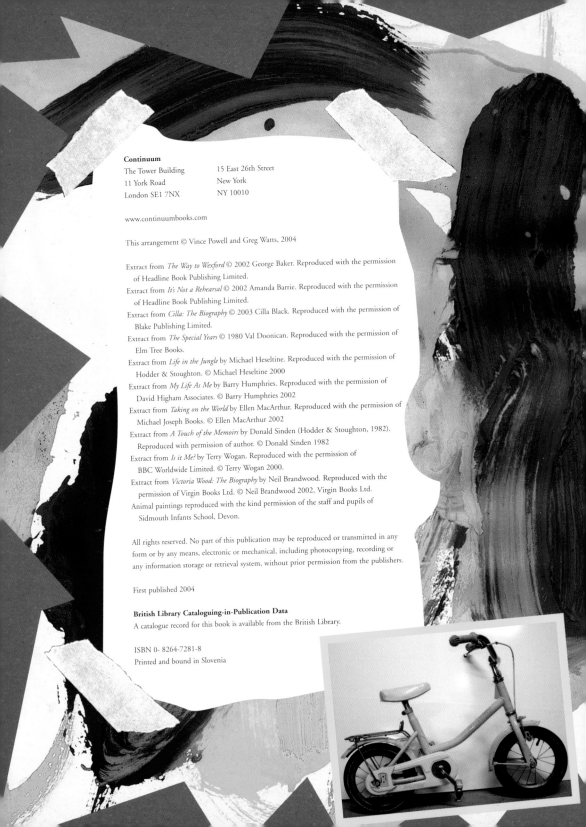

Continuum

The Tower Building   15 East 26th Street
11 York Road   New York
London SE1 7NX   NY 10010

www.continuumbooks.com

This arrangement © Vince Powell and Greg Watts, 2004

First published 2004

British Library Cataloguing-in-Publication Data
A catalogue record for this book is available from the British Library.

ISBN 0- 8264-7281-8
Printed and bound in Slovenia

List of Contributors

Foreword
Michael Aspel

Introduction
Vince Powell and Gregg Watts

Memories

Michael Aspel
George Baker
Amanda Barrie
Amanda Berry
Cilla Black
Tony Blair
Rabbi Lionel Blue
Charles Collingwood
Terence Conran
Ken Dodd
Val Doonican
Joel Edwards (Evangelical Alliance)
Jonathan Edwards
Bill Frindall
Michael Grade
Archbishop Gregorios of Thyateira
  and Great Britain
Michael Heseltine
Archbishop David Hope
Michael Howard
Barry Humphries
David Jason
Barabara Kelly
Charles Kennedy
David Lodge
Ellen MacArthur
Sir Cameron Mackintosh

Don MacLean
Sally Magnusson
Beverley Malone
Mike McClean
Sir John Mills
Sir Patrick Moore
Sir Roger Moore
Cardinal Cormac Murphy-
  O'Connor
Rt Rev'd Vincent Nichols
Tom O'Connor
William Roache
Bill Samuel
Brian Sewell
Clare Short
Sir Donald Sinden
Carol Smilie
Peter Stanford
Meera Syal
Chris Tarrant
Alan Titchmarsh
June Whitfield
Sir Norman Wisdom
Terry Wogan
Victoria Wood
Anthony Worrall-Thompson
Benjamin Zephania

Foreword

This will possibly not be the first anthology of childhood recollections you have come across, early memories remain vivid and the emotions we feel as children are as strong as anything that we feel later – joy, despair, love, and a need for friendship and fair play.

The contributors to this selection are as varied a bunch as you could imagine. One or two are so exalted that it is difficult to believe that they actually had a childhood. But that's what binds us together, of course, we all went through it, and these accounts, touching, hilarious and fascinating, should ring a bell in every reader's mind and heart.

The NSPCC will make sure that the proceeds from this book will help to enhance the lives of young people who are in sore need of a few happy memories.

MICHAEL ASPEL
9 March, 2004.

Andrew Olney

NSPCC
Cruelty to children must stop. FULL STOP.

National Society for the Prevention of
Cruelty to Children

Weston House
42 Curtain Road
London EC2A 3NH

Telephone: 020 7825 2500
Fax: 020 7825 2525

Family holidays are my happiest memories of childhood. My father was a GP and ran his practice in our family home so we shared the house with around 200 strangers every week. The telephone also never stopped ringing. It was good to get away. We would leave before dawn and get ahead of the traffic. My mother kept the peace between me and my brother, my two sisters and our dog Ross.

We usually went to Scotland or the Lake District in the mountains or by the sea. This is where I learnt my love of walking and the joy of empty sandy beaches in all weathers. Sandcastles were my father's particular speciality with intricate tunnels and bridges to allow different routes for golf balls that all started off together from the top. We were highly competitive.

On wet days we would have races to complete jigsaws, play cards or board games, and read endless novels a passion I still have today. When I swam in the Mediterranean for the first time I was surprised by how warm it was! The best day every summer was my birthday - I used to recite all the different places where I had been for each one.

Mary Marsh

NSPCC
CHILD PROTECTION
HELPLINE
0808 800 5000

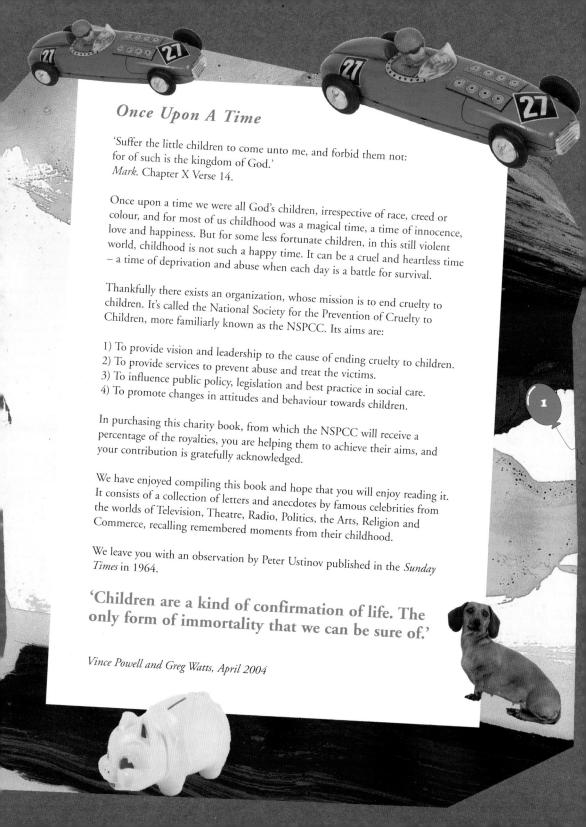

Once Upon A Time

'Suffer the little children to come unto me, and forbid them not: for of such is the kingdom of God.'
Mark. Chapter X Verse 14.

Once upon a time we were all God's children, irrespective of race, creed or colour, and for most of us childhood was a magical time, a time of innocence, love and happiness. But for some less fortunate children, in this still violent world, childhood is not such a happy time. It can be a cruel and heartless time – a time of deprivation and abuse when each day is a battle for survival.

Thankfully there exists an organization, whose mission is to end cruelty to children. It's called the National Society for the Prevention of Cruelty to Children, more familiarly known as the NSPCC. Its aims are:

1) To provide vision and leadership to the cause of ending cruelty to children.
2) To provide services to prevent abuse and treat the victims.
3) To influence public policy, legislation and best practice in social care.
4) To promote changes in attitudes and behaviour towards children.

In purchasing this charity book, from which the NSPCC will receive a percentage of the royalties, you are helping them to achieve their aims, and your contribution is gratefully acknowledged.

We have enjoyed compiling this book and hope that you will enjoy reading it. It consists of a collection of letters and anecdotes by famous celebrities from the worlds of Television, Theatre, Radio, Politics, the Arts, Religion and Commerce, recalling remembered moments from their childhood.

We leave you with an observation by Peter Ustinov published in the *Sunday Times* in 1964.

'Children are a kind of confirmation of life. The only form of immortality that we can be sure of.'

Vince Powell and Greg Watts, April 2004

It is December 23, 1935. I am two years eleven months and twelve days old.

My father appears by my bed and whispers 'Come and see what Father Christmas has brought us.' He carries me into another room, where I am introduced to my brand-new brother Alan. I am very disappointed, I have been hoping for a nice set of building bricks.

My next clear memory of Alan is nearly five years later. His fat little legs are clambering up the steps of Earlsfield railway station in South West London. Like me and our big sister Pat he is wearing a label and carrying a gas mask. World War II has begun, and we are evacuees, off to the safety of the country, far away from the threat of German bombers.

Pat and Alan were billetted with a pair of genteel spinster ladies, while I was placed in the care of a married couple who seemed elderly to me, but were probably in their late forties. Uncle Cyril and Aunt Rose gave me almost total freedom, and I was soon rampaging happily through the fields of Somerset. After a while Alan's foster parents decided that I was a little too rough for their liking, and I was instructed to keep my distance. I remember standing outside their neat detached house, shouting "I want to see my brother." We still saw each other at school, of course, when I did my eight-year-old best to corrupt him.

There were two cinemas in Chard – the Regent and the Cerdic. I adored the pictures and went at least twice a week, always re-enacting the main feature afterwards, with myself in the leading role (I did a particularly good Hopalong Cassidy). When *Gone With The Wind* came to town, Uncle Cyril told me that queues had been forming outside the Cerido at 9.30 in the morning. The next day I was there at nine sharp, my two pennies at the ready. By the time the doors opened at a quarter to two I had been joined by three old ladies and a dog, and the coppers had turned my fingers green.

Hollywood and all things American represented the ultimate in glamour and excitement to a scruffy little boy in shorts and Fairisle jumper, and I dreamed of the day I would go there. As it turned out, America came to me. One day my pal Albie Mallows announced that a mass of tents and other temporary buildings had suddenly appeared in fields just outside the town. The US army had arrived. We descended or them like a band of freckle-faced Mohicans, circling the camp and whooping until they finally let us in. From that moment until the day they left we spent all our spare time with them, explaining our currency, running their errands, becoming their friends and mascots. They found our situation as evacuees difficult to comprehend. One of them, whose name was Philip Demopoulos, wanted to know if my parents would allow me to go to live in the States, which earned him a wistful smile.

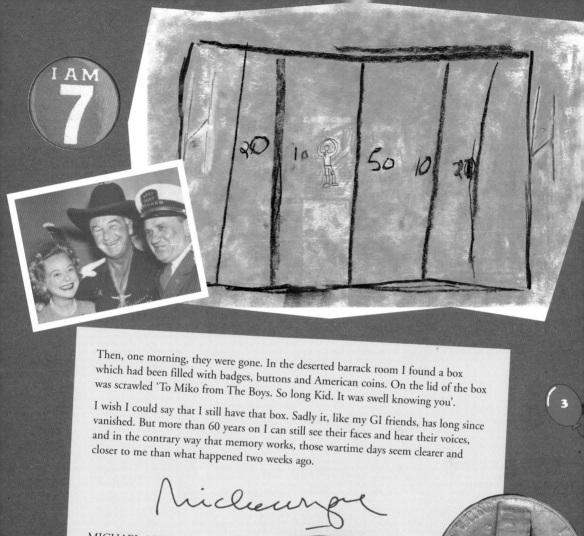

Then, one morning, they were gone. In the deserted barrack room I found a box which had been filled with badges, buttons and American coins. On the lid of the box was scrawled 'To Miko from The Boys. So long Kid. It was swell knowing you'.

I wish I could say that I still have that box. Sadly it, like my GI friends, has long since vanished. But more than 60 years on I can still see their faces and hear their voices, and in the contrary way that memory works, those wartime days seem clearer and closer to me than what happened two weeks ago.

MICHAEL ASPEL

Even family holidays were not allowed to be merely holidays for me. The clue came when Mummy packed. She always took my dance costumes, my tap shoes and my music. The bucket and spade came last, not that I had much time for them. We entered every seaside competition going and I remember only too well the lengths to which she would go . . .

In Llandudno there was a crisis when Mummy discovered that she had forgotten to take my sheet music for 'I Am Just a Little Girl Who's Looking For a Little Boy to Love', the Gershwin song, which was my current party piece. She soon found a solution, though. She simply walked into the middle of a full orchestra rehearsal on the pier and stopped it. There were hundreds of musicians there. I believe the orchestra was the Welsh Philharmonic but that did not faze my mother one little bit. She just strode up to the conductor (whom I later learned was John Monarva, who was quite well known then) and said 'Excuse me. I have a terrible problem. My daughter hasn't got her music. Could you help, please?'

He was so astonished that he did. He sat me on the piano, on the stage, and asked me to sing the song to him, then he jotted the notes down on a piece of sheet music, and underneath he wrote 'I Am Just a Little Girl'. He scribbled it all down and instructed my mother to tell whoever would be accompanying me to play the chords underneath. So up she pranced to the musicians in the talent competition I was in and they did precisely that. I won it too. I think all concerned were probably afraid what might happen if I lost.

Amanda Barrie with Hilary Bonner, *It's Not a Rehearsal: The Autobiography* (Headline, 2002). ISBN: 0753311221

I had a very happy childhood in Liverpool and never realised how poor we were until much later because everyone else was in the same boat. The barber's shop next door (via a connecting staircase) was really our front door. I remember my mother sitting on the stairs crying because the council came round to the flat and said they could do the place up. That meant we weren't getting a council house and my Mam always longed for her own front door.

My first day at school was horrendous. I couldn't understand why my mother was dumping me off at this strange place. As the only girl at home, I was spoiled and kind of clingy, so it was all extra traumatic. One of my plaits came undone and it seemed like the end of the world. I was crying, 'Please don't leave me, I don't want to go'. Though I should have been used to it, because I'd gone to nursery school.

Like my brothers, I went to St. Anthony's, a Catholic school near Scottie Road. We had to give donations for the privilege of attending and buy all our own books, pencils, everything. I was there from the age of five til I left at fifteen. Sister Marie Julie, the headmistress, was a tiny old lady, like a penguin in glasses, the terror of the school. I was always fighting to be one of the boys, but they didn't want to know – I'm still more comfortable with men than with women. But from the age of eleven we were taught separately and had different playgrounds. I was quite popular at school, very much a tomboy and always the practical joker.

At thirteen I dyed my hair with a camilia tone sevenpenny rinse from Woolworths. My Aunt Vera had auburn hair and I wanted to look like her. You were supposed to mix it with a couple of pints of water and then rinse continually over a bowl, but though I hadn't done chemistry it didn't take me long to realise that if I mixed it to a paste and painted it on with a toothbrush I'd get a much stronger colour – I left it on for hours and hours. At school next day word went round that Priscilla Maria Veronica White had gone all of a sudden from pale-blondish-mousy hair to bright red – bright orange, really. It caused an uproar in the class.

The teacher, Sister Marie Julie, sat me underneath the window where the sun shone in, which was the best thing she could have done to me. I was in the spotlight, you see, and thought it was terrific. Looking back, I must have been a dreadful child. My mother never made a fuss. I was always spoiled and I guess she thought, 'Red hair, what the hell?' It has been fair before, a really boring old colour.

Douglas Thompson, *Cilla: The Biography* (Blake Publishing Ltd, 2003).
ISBN: 1843580705

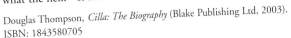

Nothing in my Bulgarian childhood could possibly have prepared me for life in England. The summers were hot and the swimming was good; I learnt to swim when I was very young and my father taught me to ride when I was three.

On one of the terraces leading down from the villa grew an old fig tree. Frank and I would lie in the shade under its large leaves waiting for a ripe fig to drop into our mouths. Not a single one ever did. There were eating grapes, too, all at a good height for children to pick on their way down to the beach. There was a Turkish fountain on which floated a small blue boat and in this we sailed the seven seas. Pirates, renegade men-of-war, steel-hulled German battleships, we fought them all and won. If we stood on the fountain wall we could pick cherries from the overhanging branches. One other vivid early memory I have of myself is lying near an ants' nest, getting the ants to walk into a shallow cup, pouring water on them and drinking them. This peculiar pastime doesn't seem to have done me any harm. I think I was learning to cook.

George Baker, *The Way to Wexford: The Autobiography* (Headline, 2002). ISBN: 0747253811

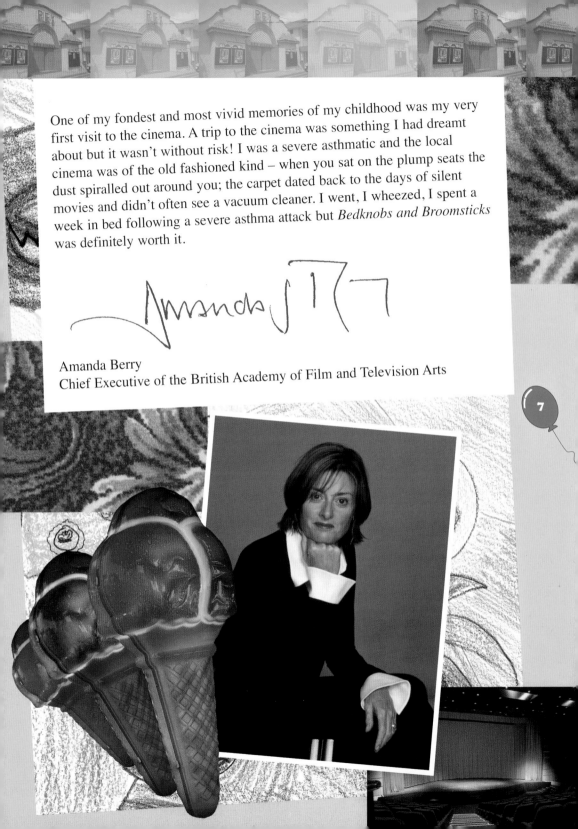

One of my fondest and most vivid memories of my childhood was my very first visit to the cinema. A trip to the cinema was something I had dreamt about but it wasn't without risk! I was a severe asthmatic and the local cinema was of the old fashioned kind – when you sat on the plump seats the dust spiralled out around you; the carpet dated back to the days of silent movies and didn't often see a vacuum cleaner. I went, I wheezed, I spent a week in bed following a severe asthma attack but *Bedknobs and Broomsticks* was definitely worth it.

Amanda Berry
Chief Executive of the British Academy of Film and Television Arts

10 DOWNING STREET
LONDON SW1A 2AA

THE PRIME MINISTER

I always think that Christmas is a special time for children. One of my earliest childhood memories is of my final Christmas in Australia where we lived while my father was lecturing at the University of Adelaide. My family's return to England meant that there would be no more Christmas afternoon walks down to the beach to eat ice-cream. The traditional image of Christmas, with its snow covered roof tops and Santa Claus dressed in a large red coat must have made little sense to me. I was soon to find out that Christmas in County Durham would be no less enjoyable and the scenery no less beautiful, but it was certainly different.

Tony Blair

THIS IS MY BELOVED SON

CHRISTMAS 1973

AUSTRALIA 7c

GEORGE HAMORI

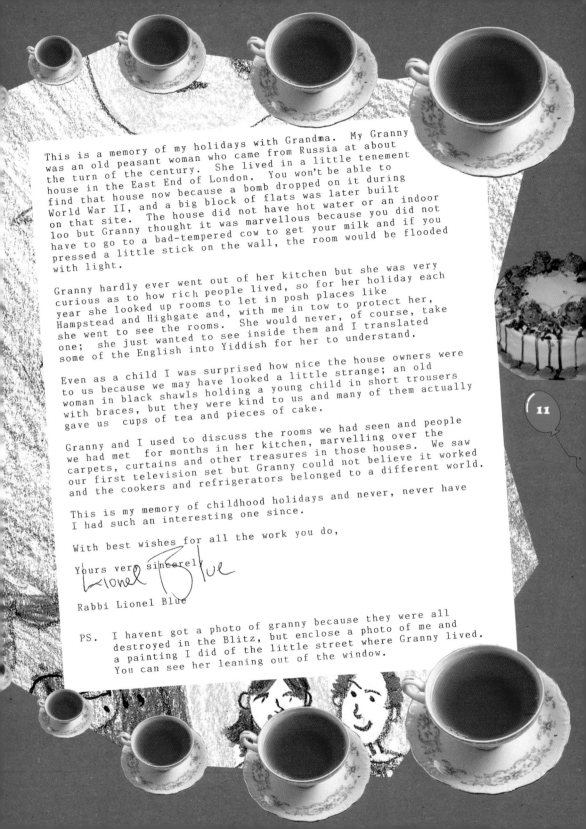

This is a memory of my holidays with Grandma. My Granny
was an old peasant woman who came from Russia at about
the turn of the century. She lived in a little tenement
house in the East End of London. You won't be able to
find that house now because a bomb dropped on it during
World War II, and a big block of flats was later built
on that site. The house did not have hot water or an indoor
loo but Granny thought it was marvellous because you did not
have to go to a bad-tempered cow to get your milk and if you
pressed a little stick on the wall, the room would be flooded
with light.

Granny hardly ever went out of her kitchen but she was very
curious as to how rich people lived, so for her holiday each
year she looked up rooms to let in posh places like
Hampstead and Highgate and, with me in tow to protect her,
she went to see the rooms. She would never, of course, take
one; she just wanted to see inside them and I translated
some of the English into Yiddish for her to understand.

Even as a child I was surprised how nice the house owners were
to us because we may have looked a little strange; an old
woman in black shawls holding a young child in short trousers
with braces, but they were kind to us and many of them actually
gave us cups of tea and pieces of cake.

Granny and I used to discuss the rooms we had seen and people
we had met for months in her kitchen, marvelling over the
carpets, curtains and other treasures in those houses. We saw
our first television set but Granny could not believe it worked
and the cookers and refrigerators belonged to a different world.

This is my memory of childhood holidays and never, never have
I had such an interesting one since.

With best wishes for all the work you do,

Yours very sincerely

Lionel Blue

Rabbi Lionel Blue

PS.   I havent got a photo of granny because they were all
      destroyed in the Blitz, but enclose a photo of me and
      a painting I did of the little street where Granny lived.
      You can see her leaning out of the window.

11

During the war when I was a child we lived near Liphook where there was a huge arms dump. The Germans rapidly discovered this and were constantly trying to bomb it.

One morning I was walking to school with my satchel over my shoulder down a country lane and I heard an outburst of machine gunfire and a huge Dormier Bomber flew very low over the tree tops with its rear gunner blazing away.

I looked him in the eye and shouted 'You can't fire at me I'm only a school boy', however he gave me a burst but missed.

I later heard that he had shot a horse in a parallel lane but missed the cart and the man leading it.

It was one of the most exciting days of my childhood and I was a hero for a day at my school.

I spent ages looking for the bullets in the lane's mossy bank and trying to find bullet holes in the trees. I never did and I now think the whole thing might have been a wartime dream.

Later the Germans saturated the area with incendiary bombs, missed the arms dump but heated up the fields around which produced the most magnificent crop of mushrooms I have ever seen.

Terence Conran

German attack on Britain

It was Christmas 1949, I was six years old and about to be a Wise Man in the school nativity play – and then my appendix went! Heartbroken, I was admitted into hospital and my appendix was skillfully dealt with, but would I be home for Christmas? Promising to be good and do as I was told I was allowed home on Christmas Eve. Tired rather than sore I wearily went upstairs to my bedroom and there beside my bed was a beautiful Christmas tree twinkling with fairy lights and coloured baubles! Happily I climbed into bed and drifted in and out of sleep glancing all the while at my very own tree. Suddenly I was woken by voices. The familiar one of my father, yes, but who did that deep rich voice belong to? 'Come in here, Charles has just come back from hospital and is in bed.'
I looked towards the door and there with my father stood Father Christmas!! I couldn't believe my eyes, Father Christmas had come personally to see me, and on Christmas Eve what's more! He put down his heavy sack, sat on the edge of my bed and asked me how I was and what I wanted for Christmas. Stutteringly, I told him. He said he'd do what he could and after a firm shake of his hand and a warm smile he was gone. But to this day I can't believe that Father Christmas really spared that precious time to come and visit me. But he did and I've never forgotten it!

Charles Collingwood

The N S P C C

January 15th 2004.

Dear Friends,

I remember well my first day at Holt High School, to which I was very pleased to have won a scholarship.

When the headmaster spoke to us all at assembly he said simply:

"Boys, you have not come here to be educated. You have come here to have your minds opened."

I have quoted this very memorable statement on several occasions. It made a great impression on me and perhaps that is one of the things that made me become a great book lover - I've got thousands of them!

Very best wishes to all those involved with your very important work.

Yours sincerely

Knotty Ash

'The Pram Crash'

'John,' I heard my mother call out, 'take that young fella downtown and get him a haircut. You'll find sixpence on the sideboard.' I hated having to go to the barbers and I know that most young lads, in those days, looked upon it much as they would a visit to the dentist.

Our local barber must have been well aware of this, since he regularly rewarded his young customers with a penny as they left the shop while patting their newly groomed heads and praising them for good behaviour and bravery in the face of danger.

I was about six years old at the time and my brothers seemed to find it a bit irritating having to match my walking pace whenever they took me out. So John decided on a plan of action that would make life a bit easier.

One of our household possessions in those days was an old pram with most unusual looking wheels. I think they were made from bamboo: like those you see on fancy tea trolleys nowadays. It was rolled onto the pavement outside the front door and I was instructed to climb aboard 'with my back to the engine' as it were. John then leaned forward taking hold of the armrests and, with his left foot resting on the axle, used the other one 'scooter style' to set us off down the road for all the world like a couple of guys starting a bob-sleigh run.

Pretty soon we were cruising along at a cracking pace. As we headed downhill towards town, John decided to jump aboard, both feet now firmly planted on the axle. I can almost feel the wonderful glow of exhilaration as the wind whizzed past my ears. My eyes however, remained glued to my brother's face as he encouraged us along with weird engine noises: Ngaaaaaaaah ... rhummmm .. rhumm .. rhumm... he whined, our craft careering down Newtown: our speed increasing by the second.

Well, I don't quite know what happened next. Maybe we bumped over a manhole, skidded on wet leaves, or my brother's enthusiasm simply reached breaking point, but suddenly that look of ecstasy which shone from his eyes turned to one of sheer panic as he somehow lost his foothold. His feet hit the road just behind our speeding vehicle, causing his head to shoot forward into the pit of my stomach. In desperation he tried to hold on—but in vain. I watched the back of his head as it went sliding over my knees, then his chin slowly pulled my socks down to my ankles till finally, with one last desperate lurch, he was gone. I just left him, lying spread-eagled in the middle of the road, as my machine and I sped on down the hill, 'driverless'.

You can just imagine my situation! I had no earthly way of stopping the thing. I couldn't turn round to see where I was going. In fact, I was so completely petrified that I sat absolutely motionless except for my eyeballs, which flashed from side to side, first to the left, then the right, exchanging glances with each passer-by. One by one, people stopped in their tracks, slowly turned round on the spot, and stared speechless as I flashed by and disappeared into the distance.

Now, local knowledge told me that at the bottom of the hill, the wall of our city park skirted the road. It was a very low wall and I'd quickly worked out that, from the angle at which my vehicle was moving, the park wall would indeed be my final destination. I didn't bother to shout for help. In fact, by now, I had simply accepted that I was about to reach my final end at the age of six and a half, the victim of a pram crash.

And what a pram crash it turned out to be! When at last the front wheels hit the kerb the pram simply leaped into the air and with a sickening thud, collided with the wall. I, in turn, took off from my seat and headfirst, went slithering over the park wall, disappearing down the other side like a snake down a hole. I landed, headfirst on a cinder covered walkway and for a moment all was still, as I lay there in a daze, my poor scalp tingling from the effects of the cinders.

'Are y' alright boy?' John whispered, as he leaned over me, gently helping me to my feet. I don't know if I answered but do know that, shortly afterwards, I was seated on a little plank of wood perched across the armrests of the barbers chair (for the benefit of the 'little people') each stroke of the comb and snip of the scissors bringing tears to my eyes. My brother sat on the bench behind me watching the refection of my agonies in the mirror. Whenever I took a peek and caught his eye, he would smile a wicked smile, slowly raising a threatening fist as if to say, 'Don't you dare say it hurts or we'll both get into trouble, and what's more, you wont get your penny.'

At the risk of sounding smug, I think I should inform you that I sat through the entire ordeal without a whimper; I got my reward sure enough and have never told a soul about the incident until now. Mind you, I think the pram was a write-off.

Val Doonican

The Special Years (Elm Tree Books, 1980). ISBN: 0241104998

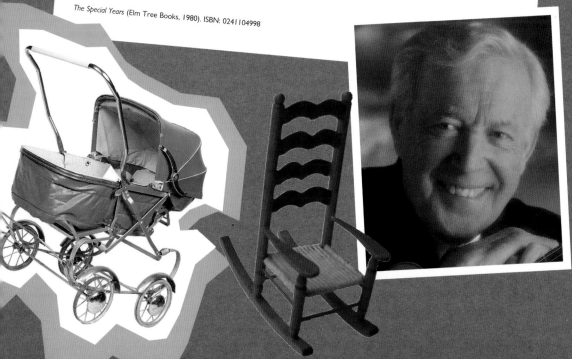

To the NSPCC

I want to tell you about my earliest childhood memory. We lived in Bristol, and my parents' flat backed onto open land which was being developed. It was full of construction equipment of all varieties, and was a complete wonderland for a young boy of 3½ years. I used to sit on the back wall and watch the scene for hours, entirely enthralled. There is a slightly sad postscript, though, as I was offered a ride on one of the JCBs by one of the drivers who had noticed my fascination. Needless to say, I was far too scared, and refused! And so now I always encourage my children to make the most of every opportunity that comes their way.

Yours sincerely,

[signature]

NSPCC
c/o Continuum
Freepost LON15713
London
SE1 7YZ

Dear NSPCC

Re: Once Upon a Time

May has always been something of a trigger month for me. That's because I got married in May but there's another reason.

In May 1960 I left Jamaica with two sisters to join my mother in Britain. I was eight years old but I remember it as though it was yesterday!

I can still smell the new fabric of my brand-new short trouser sailor suit and the squeeze of my new shoes as my uncle kneeled down to put them on. And I bawled! I was in the middle of mayhem surrounded by adults and friends I was about to be torn away from forever. I thought my life was at an end. That morning, I cried forever.

And I remember my uncle asking, "What yu cryin' fa bwoy?" It must have been the most stupid question in the world – ever! "I'm gonna miss my friends!" I sprayed.   He said, "Ahh! Friends easy to get, man!" I didn't believe him.

I remember slipping into the leather seat of his black Hillman Minx for the long road to the airport in Kingston and climbing the steps to the massive silver British Overseas Airways Corporation plane. And I remember the man who sat next to me going ballistic as the smoke shot from the propellers when the engines shook into life. "Lord Jesus!" the big man cried, "The plane catch fire!" And I remember the nice White lady with the uniform who calmed him down and said it always did that. It wasn't a great start.

And even now I can see myself sampling tasteless food as I sat in the humming womb of the great bus roaring above the clouds.

Then I reached Heathrow to see my mum. And as I walked shakily down the clanging steps to the tarmac, for the first time in my life, I saw a sun in the sky I couldn't feel on my skin.

My mother cried. It had been two years; I wasn't sure yet who she was.

20

Another uncle drove me to my new home in Kentish Town in London. It seemed like a long way. And when I came to my new home I was quite sure they had taken me to a factory. For as far as my eyes could see, all the houses were stuck together and they all looked exactly alike.

I thought my home would be a cottage, with snow and a robin redbreast on the gatepost – just like the Christmas cards my mother sent.

When they closed the door behind me, the day stopped.

That was all a long time ago and what then felt like the longest day has turned out to be an exciting, lifelong discovery. And guess what? My uncle was right after all: I found new and very different friends.

Yours sincerely

Joel

JOEL EDWARDS
General Director

21

BRINGS FARAWAY PLACES NEAR

Surrey County Cricket Club

Dear Sirs,

My most vivid childhood memory concerns an event which was to shape the rest of my life.

Games afternoon was the highlight of the week at Tadworth County Primary School in rural Surrey, especially during the cricket season. The pitch had been hewn from the vast bracken covered heath which surrounded the small school on three sides. As rain lashed the classroom windows one May morning in 1950, the games field presented a dismal sight to children who had been counting the minutes to their release into fresh air.

Jack Glenister was in his first year as a teacher after been fast-tracked through his training on a special scheme available to demobbed servicemen. Neither that training nor his wartime service in the RAF had prepared him for the ordeal of keeping 30 eight to eleven-year-olds amused for an entire afternoon. What saved him was his love of cricket, he opened the batting for Epsom, and his knowledge of cricket scoring. He had spotted a minute scorebook in the stationery cupboard. Removing the staples, he separated the tiny pages and gave one set to each of us. He had already chalked a sample page on the blackboard and for the next two hours we painstaking scored an imaginary match, ball by ball and dot by dot. Probably only three of us would remember that lesson, the others being Stewart Storey who went on to become a key all-rounder for Surrey and Sussex and that inspired teacher.

We were living opposite to a cricket ground at Kingswood and, four days later I sought refuge there to escape my parents' weekly shopping expedition to Croydon. The players were practicing when I arrived. One of them spotted me and I thought he was going to tell me I was trespassing on the private property of the Legal and General Assurance Society, which I was. He astonished me by asking if I knew how to score. Relieved, I told him I had been taught at school that Tuesday afternoon. His expression of incredulity remains vividly etched. No one is ever formally taught to score. Most would be sat next to an experienced opposition scorer and learn on the hoof. Dubiously he introduced me to the team, gave me the batting order and the scorebook and paved the way for me to become BBC radio's scorer/statistician 16 years later.

From the first time he heard me on 'Test Match Special' Jack Glenister dined out on being the man who had taught Bill Frindall to score. He lived to his late eighties and I cherish my memories of our annual lunches in Epsom.

Yours sincerely,

Bill Frindall

Although in later life I made a decent living out of the flickering television screen, my first love was radio, or to be historically more accurate, the wireless. I was born in 1943, so my pre-teen years were filled with the outpourings of "the BBC Light Programme". At home I had a set by my bed, complete with valves which took an age to warm up, but which then gave me access to hours of laughs and fun. The highlights of my week were "Ray's A Laugh", with Ted Ray and Kitty Blewitt (loved that name), "Life with the Lyons", Bebe, Ben and their children Richard and Barbara, "Up the Pole" with Jimmy Jewell and Ben Warriss (or Jules and his walrus as Eric Morecambe later dubbed them!) and "Take It From Here", with Professor Jimmy Edwards. There was something mystical and magical lying in bed, my ear pressed to the speaker (everyone thought I was asleep), sharing the laughs with the unseen studio audience. "Ignorance Is Bliss" was another favourite, Stewart MacPherson hosting a sort on surreal idiots' non-brains trust with a cast of characters – Gladys Morgan and Harold Berens are the only two panellists I can remember. Hilarious stuff all, but I daren't laugh too loud lest my secret listening after lights out be discovered – and thus curtailed. Later, I moved on to some drama, "The Archers", "Mrs Dale's Diary" and, scary even to think of, "Journey Into Space". My family were all in the entertainment business, so I suppose it was inevitable I would follow suit. But somehow, if I hadn't spent those formative years in the dark, glued to the BBC, I would never have developed my passion for comedy, comedians and entertainment.

MICHAEL GRADE

25

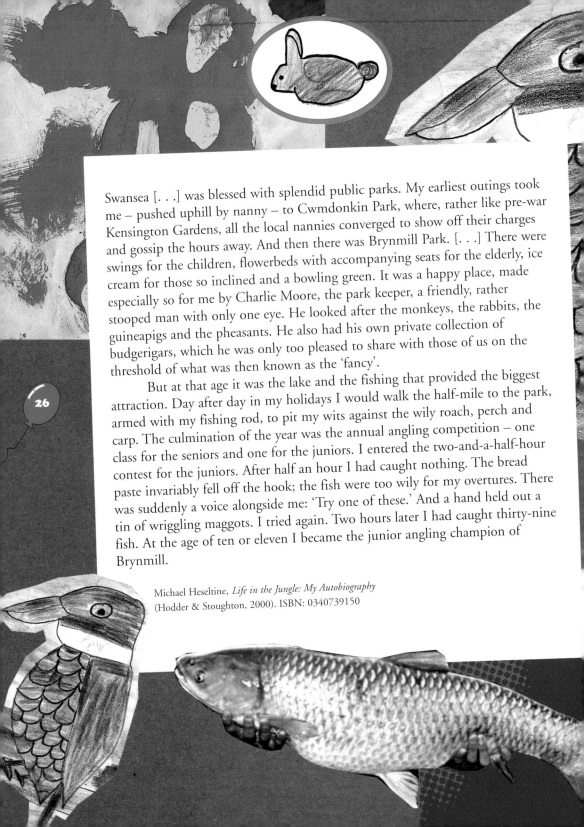

Swansea [. . .] was blessed with splendid public parks. My earliest outings took me – pushed uphill by nanny – to Cwmdonkin Park, where, rather like pre-war Kensington Gardens, all the local nannies converged to show off their charges and gossip the hours away. And then there was Brynmill Park. [. . .] There were swings for the children, flowerbeds with accompanying seats for the elderly, ice cream for those so inclined and a bowling green. It was a happy place, made especially so for me by Charlie Moore, the park keeper, a friendly, rather stooped man with only one eye. He looked after the monkeys, the rabbits, the guineapigs and the pheasants. He also had his own private collection of budgerigars, which he was only too pleased to share with those of us on the threshold of what was then known as the 'fancy'.

But at that age it was the lake and the fishing that provided the biggest attraction. Day after day in my holidays I would walk the half-mile to the park, armed with my fishing rod, to pit my wits against the wily roach, perch and carp. The culmination of the year was the annual angling competition – one class for the seniors and one for the juniors. I entered the two-and-a-half-hour contest for the juniors. After half an hour I had caught nothing. The bread paste invariably fell off the hook; the fish were too wily for my overtures. There was suddenly a voice alongside me: 'Try one of these.' And a hand held out a tin of wriggling maggots. I tried again. Two hours later I had caught thirty-nine fish. At the age of ten or eleven I became the junior angling champion of Brynmill.

Michael Heseltine, *Life in the Jungle: My Autobiography*
(Hodder & Stoughton, 2000). ISBN: 0340739150

ΟΙΚΟΥΜΕΝΙΚΟΝ
ΠΑΤΡΙΑΡΧΕΙΟΝ

ECUMENICAL
PATRIARCHATE

ΙΕΡΑ ΑΡΧΙΕΠΙΣΚΟΠΗ ΘΥΑΤΕΙΡΩΝ ΚΑΙ ΜΕΓΑΛΗΣ ΒΡΕΤΑΝΙΑΣ
ARCHDIOCESE OF THYATEIRA AND GREAT BRITAIN

5th January 2004

Dear Friends,

Thank you for the recent letter inviting me to contribute a childhood memory to the charity book that is to be published on your behalf by Continuum International Publishing.

I am happy to participate and enclose a short account entitled "*The Day the Circus came to Town*", which I hope that you will find it suitable for your purposes. I also enclose a colour photograph of myself, as requested. I regret that I do not have one that dates from my childhood.

THE DAY THE CIRCUS CAME TO TOWN

It was a great day in the village in which I was born in Cyprus more than seventy years ago. Even though we lived some way from the capital, Nicosia, we still liked to think of ourselves as being progressive and not too far behind the city-dwellers. And this view was reinforced when one of the villagers, who many years previously had emigrated to New Zealand, returned home and opened a coffee-shop – which quickly became one of the village's principal meeting points.

Hearing that a circus would be visiting Nicosia, he arranged for it to come to the village as well. You can imagine the excitement of both young and old as the circus rolled into town with its caravans and the cages housing wild animals – the like of which we had never seen before. The big top was quickly put up and tickets went on sale for a very limited number of performances. We children were particularly excited, and we followed the activities of the exotic circus folk with ever-increasing interest.

I was the youngest in the family. My father had died when I was very small, and my eldest brother was now head of the household. As far as I can remember, tickets for the circus were only a halfpenny (½p). So, I approached my mother and asked if I could have the money, adding that the teacher of my class at school had said that we all ought to go.

We were not a wealthy family and I had a lot of brothers and sisters. Mother did her best to look after us all – something which she did extremely well, with the result that there always seemed to be something left over for those less fortunate than ourselves. I therefore felt that we could easily afford the halfpenny for me to go to the circus.

My mother was ready to give me the money, but my brother (of blessed memory) was not in agreement. He said, "No", and explained that, in fact, we had very little money and that however small a sum a halfpenny might

seem, it would mean that something else more essential would have to be gone without. I looked at my mother, hoping for her support. But she smiled with that particular smile of hers and shook her head. However, I knew that she agreed with me, but that she did not want to do something that would upset my brother. Any thought of going to the circus would therefore have to be forgotten.

It was a hard lesson and one which was very difficult for someone of my age. However, it taught me that we cannot always have all the things we would like in life. And, of course, my mother made up for my disappointment in other ways.

Today, my village, Marathovounos near Famagusta, is occupied by a foreign power and its families have been dispersed. The church stands empty and its bells no longer ring out to remind us of the Good News of our Salvation. And what's more, whenever I see a circus advertised, not only does the memory of my village and the circus that visited it come rushing back but I am reminded of that difficult lesson that I learnt all those years ago.

With best wishes and New Year blessings

Gregorios
Archbishop of Thyateira
and Great Britain

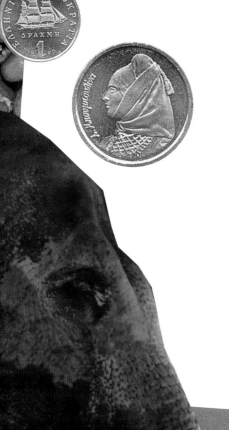

29

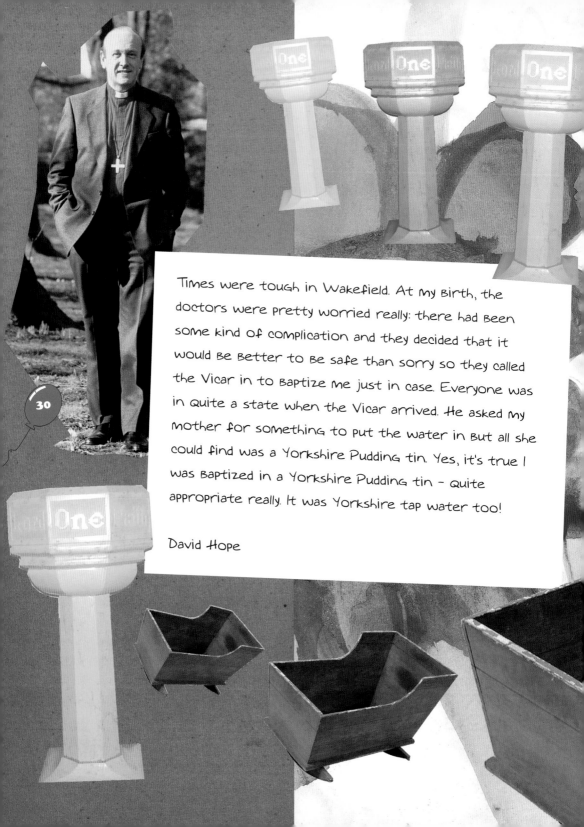

Times were tough in Wakefield. At my Birth, the doctors were pretty worried really: there had been some kind of complication and they decided that it would be better to be safe than sorry so they called the Vicar in to baptize me just in case. Everyone was in quite a state when the Vicar arrived. He asked my mother for something to put the water in but all she could find was a Yorkshire Pudding tin. Yes, it's true I was baptized in a Yorkshire Pudding tin - quite appropriate really. It was Yorkshire tap water too!

David Hope

The Happiest Day of My Life

An awesome day at my friends' house;
I could taste the excitement in my mouth.
As we left the school behind,
We played games.
There was a lot of fame,
We jumped in the pool,
It was so cool!
We went up the steep stairs,
We crept in their creepy lair;
We made a pretend fire,
We sang like a choir;
We played Grand Turismo 3 at my Friends house.

My Hopes for the Future

In the future I hope for peace,
War and hatred forever ceased,
I hope to sing in my career;
I hope my life flows very clear;
And keep my happiness ever near;
In the future.

By Sean Age 9

THE RT HON MICHAEL HOWARD QC MP

HOUSE OF COMMONS
LONDON SW1A 0AA

LEADER OF THE OPPOSITION

The NSPCC
Weston House,
42 Curtain Road,
London EC2A 3NH

4 February 2004

Dear Mr Bird-Smith

Childhood Memories

My earliest childhood memory is as follows.

I clearly remember seeing Field Marshal Montgomery on a visit to Llanelli to celebrate our victory in the Second World War. As I recall it, he was sitting in the back of a jeep saluting the cheering crowds lining the streets. It was a great moment of shared pride.

Yours sincerely
Michael Howard.

MICHAEL HOWARD

Perhaps the most horrible gift I ever received from my father, apart from a cricket bat, was a pair of boxing gloves.

'It's important that Barry learns how to defend himself', he said, although he never mentioned against whom. I had a brief vision of all those people out there waiting to hit me. I was not ten years of age and yet my father, normally a gentle man, was taking a bloodthirsty pleasure in organizing backyard boxing matches in which I was expected to spar with neighbourhood boys. We had been taught the rudiments of boxing by Scottie, the bald bully who ran the gymnasium at my junior school, Camberwell Grammar, but I detested it then, and what still seems to me now to be a perfectly natural aversion to pain and facial injury earnt me the shaming nickname of 'Granny Humphries'. Whenever I was thrown into a ring with some keen young lout, I always concentrated on losing the match without loss of blood.

The backyard boxing matches were short-lived. My mother put a stop to them forever after I gave Graham Coles a bloody nose, by accident rather than design. The poor boy fled home in tears, a crimson handkerchief pressed to his face, but I was ashamed to observe my father's mood of quiet triumph. Was this what was expected of me? I wondered. Was this what it took to be a real man?

Barry Humphries, *My Life as Me: A Memoir* (Michael Joseph, 2002). ISBN: 0718145410

34

The Happiest Moment of My Life

The happiest moment of my life was when we went to Florida, and we met Minnie and Mickey Mouse. We went to the Magic Kingdom. I had a picture with Tarzan, Mowgli, Pinocchio and Timone. It was so much fun! We went to Epcot, the Animal Kingdom! We saw the Midnight Parade and the castle lit up and changed colours and the floats were amazing!

My Hopes for the Future

To become a doctor or a member of the RSPCA and make animals be nursed to health. Next year I am hoping to go on holiday to the Magic Kingdom and see it all again!

By Emily Age 10

January, 2004

Once Upon A Time for the NSPCC

I was about 11 years old and, if it hadn't have been for a boy in my class who contracted the measles, I would never have been an actor.

He was playing a leading role in the school play and they needed someone to take his place. The idea of acting was for us boys, a very sissy thing to do and so none of us butch boys would volunteer. When the Headmaster came up to me and asked me to take the part, I politely refused. He then said "let me put it this way young man, don't make me tell you to do it." By the time I worked out what he meant, I was doing the play and when I heard that first wave of laughter from the audience, my future was sealed.

Good luck,

DAVID JASON O.B.E.

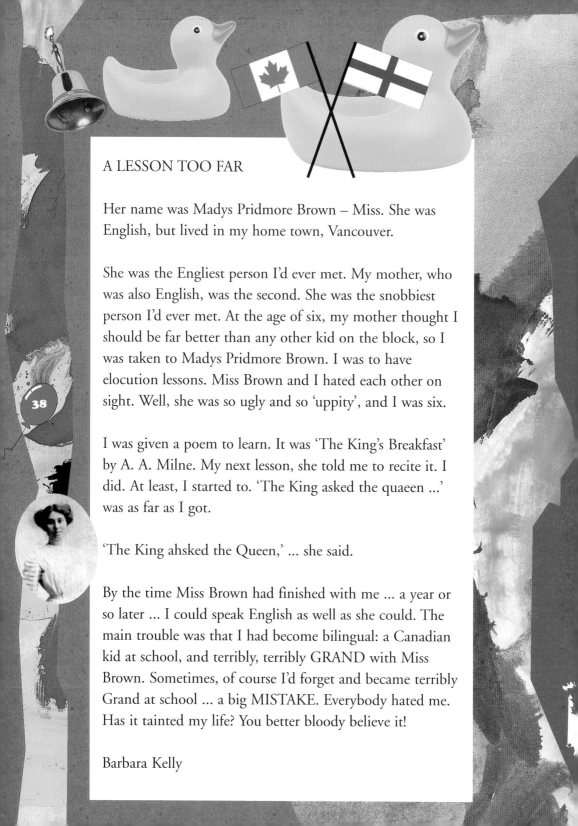

A LESSON TOO FAR

Her name was Madys Pridmore Brown – Miss. She was English, but lived in my home town, Vancouver.

She was the Engliest person I'd ever met. My mother, who was also English, was the second. She was the snobbiest person I'd ever met. At the age of six, my mother thought I should be far better than any other kid on the block, so I was taken to Madys Pridmore Brown. I was to have elocution lessons. Miss Brown and I hated each other on sight. Well, she was so ugly and so 'uppity', and I was six.

I was given a poem to learn. It was 'The King's Breakfast' by A. A. Milne. My next lesson, she told me to recite it. I did. At least, I started to. 'The King asked the quaeen ...' was as far as I got.

'The King ahsked the Queen,' ... she said.

By the time Miss Brown had finished with me ... a year or so later ... I could speak English as well as she could. The main trouble was that I had become bilingual: a Canadian kid at school, and terribly, terribly GRAND with Miss Brown. Sometimes, of course I'd forget and became terribly Grand at school ... a big MISTAKE. Everybody hated me. Has it tainted my life? You better bloody believe it!

Barbara Kelly

38

39

SPUTNIK 1

HOUSE OF COMMONS
LONDON SW1A 0AA

22nd January 2004

Dear NSPCC,

I was brought up on a croft in the West Highlands. I spent a lot of my pre-school early childhood with my grandfather surrounded by all sorts of animals, particularly hens, horses, cows and dogs: all very exciting and adventurous for a young boy. But my most enduring memories are those of the night skies.

On mild summer nights I would lie in nearby fields and look up to the clear night sky, letting my imagination run wild, wondering if there was someone else out there like me, who was looking at planet earth from the heavens above! This interest in the stars culminated in my fascination with the Apollo Moonshoot programme and the mission to the moon. I am now particularly interested by discussion of a 'moon base' which I sometimes hear being mooted.

Twenty years on and now spending much of my time in London, I do sometimes long to return to those youthful carefree days and starry nights in the West Highlands.

Yours sincerely,

The Rt. Hon. Charles Kennedy MP

40

One's earliest memories are not usually the most dramatic – often, indeed, they concern very trivial events – but they have a special fascination, as marking the boundary between the lost world of infancy and the formation of an individual consciousness – the 'autobiographical self' which we continue to construct and edit for the rest of our lives.

I was born in January, 1935, in Dulwich, south London, the first and (as it turned out) only child of my parents. When I was one year old they moved a few miles to Brockley, where they had bought a newly-built house. The location was chosen because the all-night trams passed nearby, and my father was a dance musician by profession, usually returning from work in the early hours of the morning. It was a cramped two-and-a-half bedroomed house, on the very lowest rung of owner-occupier gentility, but it was at the end of a terrace, so it had the amenity of a side-alley and a back gate, giving access to a garden with a patch of grass about three yards by sit, rimmed by a narrow concrete path. Roses, trained to grow along the wooden fences that separated us from our neighbours, flourished in the clayey soil, and afforded some privacy. Apart from interruptions caused by the Second World War, this was my parents' home until they died, and my own until I was a young man.

It is the War that allows me to identify my earliest memories. My father enlisted in the Royal Air Force soon after war was declared (not out of patriotic motives, but to ensure that he could serve as a musician) and my mother and I lived at home until the bombing of 1940 compelled us to move to the country for safety. I have vivid memories of the Blitz (which I drew on in the first section of my novel, *Out of the Shelter*), but my earliest ones are 'pre-war'.

One is of an excursion to the seaside. It might conceivably have been in the early summer of 1939, but was more probably in the previous year, when I was three. I was in a motor car which was proceeding slowly along a road beside a beach. Possibly my father was driving, for I believe that there was a brief period of prosperity when he acquired a second-hand car. It was a bright sunny day and there were crowds of people on the pavements and on the sands.

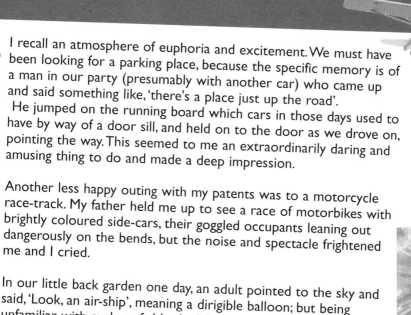

I recall an atmosphere of euphoria and excitement. We must have been looking for a parking place, because the specific memory is of a man in our party (presumably with another car) who came up and said something like, 'there's a place just up the road'.

He jumped on the running board which cars in those days used to have by way of a door sill, and held on to the door as we drove on, pointing the way. This seemed to me an extraordinarily daring and amusing thing to do and made a deep impression.

Another less happy outing with my patents was to a motorcycle race-track. My father held me up to see a race of motorbikes with brightly coloured side-cars, their goggled occupants leaning out dangerously on the bends, but the noise and spectacle frightened me and I cried.

In our little back garden one day, an adult pointed to the sky and said, 'Look, an air-ship', meaning a dirigible balloon; but being unfamiliar with such craft I looked for a real ship in the sky, and persuaded myself that I saw one, very small because it was so high — something like the Queen Mary, with a black hull and white superstructure and three funnels, sailing across the blue sky. It was some time before I accepted that this was a delusion.

43

Soon the sky would be thronged with tethered silver-grey barrage balloons, and etched with the white vapour-trails of warplanes.

David Lodge

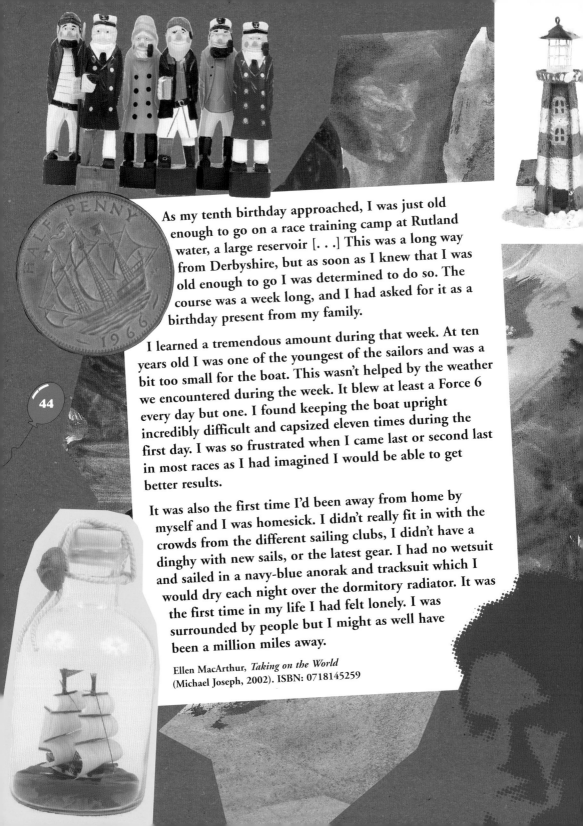

As my tenth birthday approached, I was just old enough to go on a race training camp at Rutland water, a large reservoir [. . .] This was a long way from Derbyshire, but as soon as I knew that I was old enough to go I was determined to do so. The course was a week long, and I had asked for it as a birthday present from my family.

I learned a tremendous amount during that week. At ten years old I was one of the youngest of the sailors and was a bit too small for the boat. This wasn't helped by the weather we encountered during the week. It blew at least a Force 6 every day but one. I found keeping the boat upright incredibly difficult and capsized eleven times during the first day. I was so frustrated when I came last or second last in most races as I had imagined I would be able to get better results.

It was also the first time I'd been away from home by myself and I was homesick. I didn't really fit in with the crowds from the different sailing clubs, I didn't have a dinghy with new sails, or the latest gear. I had no wetsuit and sailed in a navy-blue anorak and tracksuit which I would dry each night over the dormitory radiator. It was the first time in my life I had felt lonely. I was surrounded by people but I might as well have been a million miles away.

Ellen MacArthur, *Taking on the World* (Michael Joseph, 2002). ISBN: 0718145259

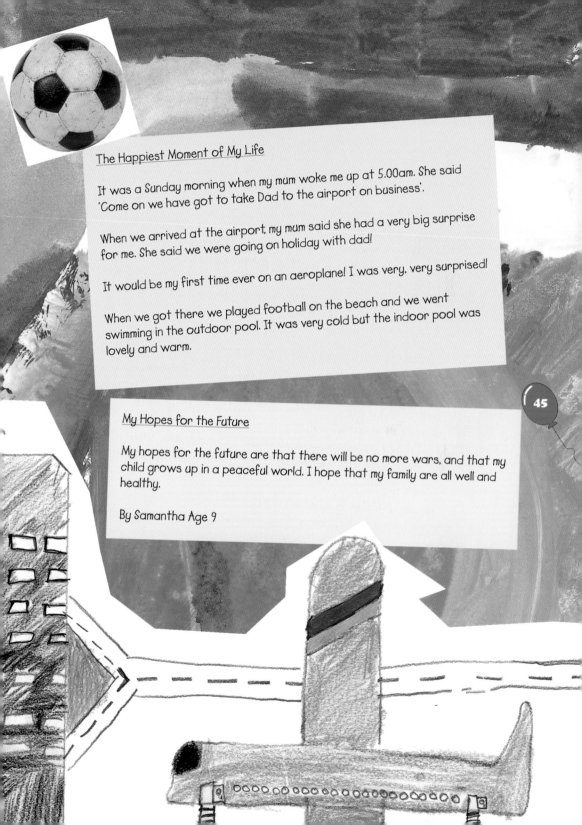

The Happiest Moment of My Life

It was a Sunday morning when my mum woke me up at 5.00am. She said 'Come on we have got to take Dad to the airport on business'.

When we arrived at the airport, my mum said she had a very big surprise for me. She said we were going on holiday with dad!

It would be my first time ever on an aeroplane! I was very, very surprised!

When we got there we played football on the beach and we went swimming in the outdoor pool. It was very cold but the indoor pool was lovely and warm.

My Hopes for the Future

My hopes for the future are that there will be no more wars, and that my child grows up in a peaceful world. I hope that my family are all well and healthy.

By Samantha Age 9

45

Nia + Benjamin

46

C A M E R O N

MACKINTOSH
L I M I T E D

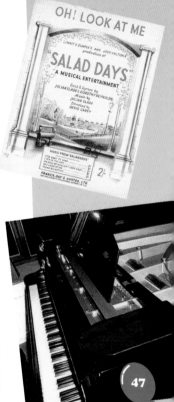

OH! LOOK AT ME

"SALAD DAYS"
A MUSICAL ENTERTAINMENT

Dear NSPCC,

I was eight, and seeing the musical *Salad Days* with its magic piano that sent London dancing.   Seeing it sent me into the theatre business....and this is how it all started. At the end of the show I was excited, not just by the piano on the stage, but by the man playing the piano in the orchestra pit.   I went down to the front of the theatre and introduced myself.   It was the show's author Julian Slade and, instead of just sending me off with a signed autograph, he took me seriously and showed me backstage. He explained how they mimed the magic piano on stage to match his playing in the orchestra pit.   He showed me how the scenery worked.   I was, as you can imagine, hooked immediately.   I decided that this was what I wanted to do when I grew up.

Over the years I have been lucky enough to be associated with several classic musicals and one of the joyous side effects of these successes has been the enormous interest children have shown not only in the songs but also in the meaning of the stories and the magic of invention which we use in the theatre to entrance the audience.

I treasure my meeting with Julian Slade and hope that over generations there have been dozens, maybe thousands, of children who have been similarly inspired to achieve their ambitions through an early theatre experience.   If any of the thousands of young people who have performed in *Oliver!* followed Oliver's example to ask for more and rebel against ill treatment, then the world will be a happier place.   If any of the thousands of young people who have worked together to stage *Les Miserables Schools Edition* decide to join in our crusade then the world will be a less selfish place.   If any of the many hundreds of thousands of young people who have been to see *Miss Saigon* think about the sacrifice that parents have to make for their future, then the world will hopefully be a better place.

I applaud the work of the NSPCC, which sadly is needed even more than ever in this tough world of ours.   The NSPCC is there to help those children who are alone, afraid and often abused.   In fact, children who never had the privilege of enjoying their Salad Days as I have.

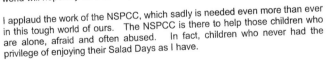

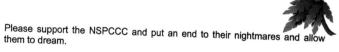

Please support the NSPCCC and put an end to their nightmares and allow them to dream.

Best wishes,

Sir Cameron Mackintosh.

47

MY CLOCK

Dear NSPPC,

I'm delighted to have been asked to contribute to 'Once Upon a Time', I just hope the following is worthy of inclusion.

There have been several unforgettable days in my life but the day on which I made my first Holy Communion was probably the first. I was up early, dressed in my suit which was a navy blue jacket with short trousers to match. I wore shirt and tie and my hair had succumbed to a generous helping of Dad's Brylcreem. We were early for nine o'clock mass but Sr Annuncia who'd prepared me for this great event was there before us, I could see her tall figure outside the church as we turned the corner into George Street. She greeted me kindly as always then delved inside her habit to find a dark red sash. She placed this over my shoulder and pinned it with a large safety pin. It had dark red tassels which banged against my hip as I walked. Once in church we were ushered into the very front pew on the right hand side. Reverend Mother was already deep in prayer, Sr Annuncia sat next to her and I was sandwiched between the large nun and my Mom who was wearing her best hat. The mass seemed interminable but eventually it came time for communion. Reverend Mother was always first to the rail to receive but this time she stood and allowed me to pass her. I knelt at the altar rail, Mom next to me and then Sr Annuncia. The altar server approached and placed the pattern under my chin. The priest stood before me, the chalice in his hand looked enormous

"Corpus Domini Nostri Jesu Christi custodiat animam tuam in vitam eternam"

"Amen" I responded and the body of Christ was placed on my tongue. A shudder passed over me causing me to raise my shoulders and arch my back. Receiving the sacrament was important and I was important, from now on I would be able to commune with God at every mass, I was a complete Catholic and suddenly I was important. Children usually make their First Communion in groups but I'd done so individually. People were waiting to shake my hand and pat my head in congratulation.

My seven year old granddaughter, Gracie, is presently preparing to make her first Holy Communion, I only hope the day remains in her memory as it has in mine.

God Bless & keep laughing!

50

553

L.M.

Fight the good fight of faith.—
1 Tim. vi. 12.

f 1 FIGHT the good fight with all thy
     might, [thy right;
   Christ is thy strength, and Christ
   Lay hold on life, and it shall be
   Thy joy and crown eternally.

mf 2 Run the straight race, through
      God's good grace, [face:
    Lift up thine eyes, and seek His
f   Life with its way before thee lies,
    Christ is the path, and Christ the
      prize.

   3 Cast care aside, upon thy Guide
     Lean, and His mercy will provide:
     Lean, and the trusting soul shall
       prove, [love.
     Christ is its life, and Christ its

f 4 Faint not, nor fear, His arms are
      near: [dear:
    He changeth not, and thou art
cr Only believe, and thou shalt see
    That Christ is all in all to thee.
                    J. S. B. MONSELL, 1863.

My childhood ended abruptly on 9 June 1973. In the blur of pain after my brother Siggy's death, I remember little except helping to choose this hymn for his funeral. Five years younger than me, the fourth child of five, he had been knocked down by a lorry as he crossed the road outside his school playing-fields a few days before his twelfth birthday.

He fought hard for life. For three days he lay in Glasgow's Western Infirmary, terribly injured but hanging on long enough for us to hope he might make it. It was that battle for life which was in our minds as we flicked through the hymn-book the next day, my mother so white and gaunt I could hardly bear to look at her, my father silently pacing backwards and forwards across the room.

51

'Fight the good fight' caught my eye, and with little more thought than that this was surely the hymn for our boy, we chose it. It was only when I rose to sing it a couple of days later in tiny Baldernock Church, stricken at the sight of the small coffin resting at the spot where parents normally stood to bring their lively children for baptism, that I realised what the rest of the hymn was telling us to do.

Amid the waste of death, we found ourselves singing 'Lay hold on life'. Deep in the misery of the sight of that still coffin, we heard ourselves murmuring, 'Lift up thine eyes'. In a haze of grief we sang of trusting to the love of Christ and a meaning to human existence where there seemed at that moment to be none at all.

Sometimes a hymn gets there before you.

Sally Magnusson *Glorious Things: Hymns for Life*, (Continuum, 2004). ISBN: 0826474179
Photograph by Derek Prescott derekprescott.photos@virgin.net

Dear NSPCC,

Thank you for this opportunity to go back into my childhood and share a treasured part of my life. I was raised principally by my great grandmother, Ms Addie, a tall, slim woman with silver grey hair and features reminiscent of an American Indian. When she was younger, her hair was red but by the time I came along, she was already sixty-five years old. So I knew her with beautiful long silver hair that she would let me plait into two long braids that hung down her back.

My Granny was a healer in our community. She always believed in feeding people in addition to bandaging a wound or administering an herbal mixture. Early in my life, I learned from her that health is holistic and includes having enough to eat, a place to sleep and the peace of mind required to focus on contributing to the world. She was and is my hero, my mentor and my inspiration for becoming a nurse.

My Granny would often take me out with her to the woods where she would replenish her medicinal supplies. She would say 'Bav—lee, (she could never pronounce my name) go get that plant, pick that leaf from there…' in her Southern accent, thick and sweet like molasses. Back home, she would mix her ingredients together and treat everything from a baby's bald head to an older adult's chronic heart condition. The baby's hair would grow and the older adult would get a new lease on a healthier lifestyle.

One of my particularly vivid memories is how my Granny got Mr George to start riding a bicycle. His feet stopped swelling, his breathing improved and the chest pains disappeared. I thought she was a miracle worker. I thought there was no one more powerful or more giving to me and to others. I decided then that I wanted to be a healer like my Granny - tall, powerful and giving to others - and that is why I came into nursing, a profession which demands that I give to others and yet receive much in return. Being a nurse keeps me close to the wonder and challenge of the lives of those we care for and also close to fine and dedicated colleagues - other nurses, midwives, doctors, physiotherapists just to name a few.

Thank you again for this opportunity. Through my Granny, and my mother, I was blessed with a childhood filled with so much love that it's still overflowing. Nursing is a work of the heart, the hands and the mind. I was shaped throughout my childhood to heal and, in turn, be healed by others. My beloved Granny was a wise woman, with a generosity of spirit and soul. My best comes from her and my faults belong only to me.

Sincerely,

Beverly Malone

WINNING THE JUNIOR CLOSE UP COMPETITION

I shall never forget the night that I won the junior close up magic competition. I had been into magic for some time; in fact that's how my first steps into show business started. I had been practising my little act in my bedroom over and over again trying to think of those funny lines that would make a room full of people laugh.

I had to do a 12 minute routine in front of about 100 people, as well as the judges of the magic circle. I was about 13 at the time and had been told that I was too small to be a footballer; so Magic it was.

While all my mates were out playing football I was busy putting the final touches to my close up act and watching every comic on TV in the vain hope that there might be a funny gag that I could use. So the morning of the big day I got up early, went to school and practised a couple of the tricks on my mates. 'Wow, you're brilliant' they said – well they would, they were my mates after all. So as the school day came to a close my nerves started.

Off I went home and wasn't able to eats mum's cooking, and boy was her cooking good – after all she was Spanish and made some fantastic dishes. So off I went and packed, making sure my black trousers, white shirt, black jacket and my little bow tie were all safely in my bag. I gave mum a goodbye kiss and my dad said good luck and not to worry if I don't win. 'Remember son it's about the taking part, not the winning.' Why do parents say that? For me I really wanted to win. I had been practising for ages and ages.

My parents were not well off so I had to get the bus into town and then one into Moston. I got there, unpacked, and we drew straws as to who went on first. Me, I was on fifth (my lucky number). My nerves were really bad – you would've seen my hands shaking from space. 'Our next young magician is a young man all the way from Levenshulme who says he loves magic and Man City. Will you please welcome on stage Mike McClean' . . . and on I went.

There was a silence that for me seemed forever. 'Good evening ladies and gentlemen. Tonight . . . ' and off I went into my routine. I had made my act last no longer than ten minutes, thus allowing for applause and laughter. Guess what – I got both. So as I left the stage I felt wonderful, as if I could do it all again. Apart from a few little snags everything went well – mind you so did the other seven acts.

'The winner of the very first junior magic circle competition here in Manchester is . . . ,

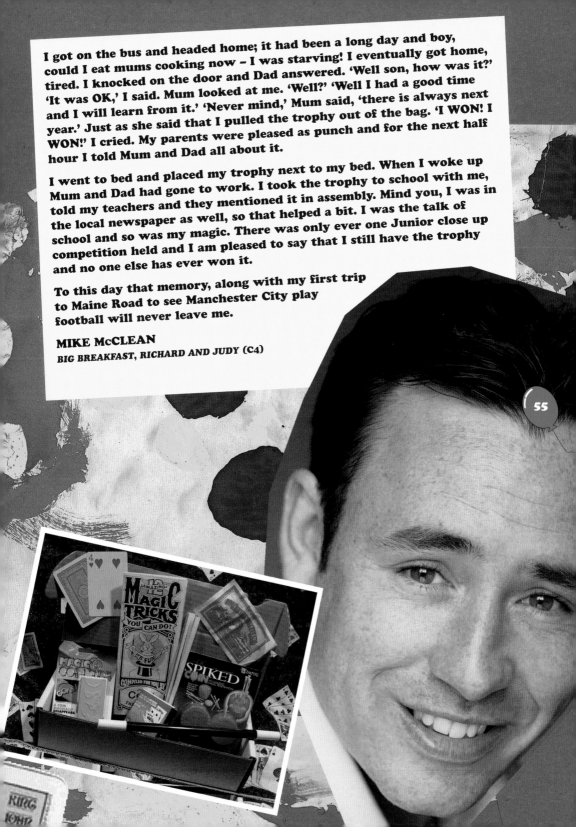

I got on the bus and headed home; it had been a long day and boy, could I eat mums cooking now – I was starving! I eventually got home, tired. I knocked on the door and Dad answered. 'Well son, how was it?' 'It was OK,' I said. Mum looked at me. 'Well?' 'Well I had a good time and I will learn from it.' 'Never mind,' Mum said, 'there is always next year.' Just as she said that I pulled the trophy out of the bag. 'I WON! I WON!' I cried. My parents were pleased as punch and for the next half hour I told Mum and Dad all about it.

I went to bed and placed my trophy next to my bed. When I woke up Mum and Dad had gone to work. I took the trophy to school with me, told my teachers and they mentioned it in assembly. Mind you, I was in the local newspaper as well, so that helped a bit. I was the talk of school and so was my magic. There was only ever one Junior close up competition held and I am pleased to say that I still have the trophy and no one else has ever won it.

To this day that memory, along with my first trip to Maine Road to see Manchester City play football will never leave me.

MIKE McCLEAN
BIG BREAKFAST, RICHARD AND JUDY (C4)

55

The Happiest Moment of My Life

The happiest moment of my life is when I moved country. Mum and Dad, Jack, Georgia and me, moved from Ireland to England because of all the war and fighting.

When we came to Poynton my Mum turned the key and opened our front door. This is where we started our new beginning.

Now that I've moved here, there's no war and there is peace. Even though I'm happy here I still miss my family. But if I lived there, fighting and war would be the only things I'd see.

So that is why the happiest moment of my life is when I moved country and came to live in England.

My Hopes for the Future

My hopes for the future are that there will be no war or fighting and no more litter or people killing each other. When I am about 25 I would like to be a car mechanic. I would like to have two children. One girl and one boy. The girl would be called Toni and the boy would be called Sam.

By Emma Age 11

SIR JOHN MILLS
Denham Village

January 19 2004

A Childhood Memory

57

I do remember with some pleasure my school summer holidays.

I used to set off with my mother, loaded with a fishing line and tackle, a box of lug worms, a bag of hundreds and thousands (very small sugary little sweets in various shapes and sizes), sandwiches, lemonade and a bathing costume.

We would walk the four and a half miles to Gorleston-on-Sea where I'd spend a blissful day fishing for dabs from the small jetty. Nine miles a day is quite a hike for a small boy of six, but the journey was shortened by an idea of my mother's; we each put one of the hundreds and thousands on our tongue and whoiever could make it last the longest was the winner.

Happy, happy days!

Sir John Mills

Sir Patrick Moore CBE FRS

December 28

LATITUDE: 50° 43' 49.25" N
LONGITUDE: 00° 41' 41.25" W

58

** ************

I am terribly sorry for muddle and delay. Usually I answer letters quickly, but everything seems to have been against me. I was ill; I have this wretched spine problem, which affects my hands and slows down my typing (hence stamp signature!) I had to cope with IV, and letters poured in. In the end, mail got completely out of control. I am battling with it now, but the pile never seems to get any smaller! With Christmas cards. I'm afraid that I have simply had to admit defeat. So - my apologies for apparent discourtesy - and Happy New Year!

****

A proud moment - at the age of 11 I was elected a member of the British Astronomical Association (an age record). I was taken to th meeting in London, and shook hands with thr Astronomer Royal as be admitted me.

That was in LOctober 1934. Exactly fifty years later, I became President!

All best wishes

Patrick Moore

R

116 Volvo 1800 S

Max. Speed   110 m.p.h. (176 km.)
B.H.P.   108 (Ch. SAE)
Comp. Ratio 10:1
              1780

DINK
TO

4¼ (105 mm.)

60

Max. Speed 150 m.p.h.
            (240 km.)
B.H.P.   282 (Ch. SAE)
Comp. Ratio 8.9:1
C.C.   3995

153 Aston Martin DB 6

DINKY

4¼ (111 mm.)

December 2003

The day I discovered there were two Father Christmas's.

Every Christmas Eve I was allowed to sleep in my parent's bed; this was for the three of us to enjoy discovering the bulging stocking at the foot of the bed on Christmas Morning.

When I was eight year's old, I was sure that Father Christmas really existed, after all how else did the stocking become filled? Actually it was not a stocking, rather one of my father's golf socks.

That particular Christmas Eve I was determined to see Father Christmas in action, I feigned sleep. I have no idea how long I lay with flickering eyelashes waiting for him to come down the chimney. I heard the door open, and my mother say that I was asleep. Little did they know! As I squinted through half closed eyes I saw my mother and father taking the sock down and replacing it with its mate, filled to the brim with packages, nuts, chocolate and an orange.

So that was it, Father Christmas was mum and dad. I considered myself very privileged; after all, I had two Father Christmas's of my very own.

I wish I had them today.

16th December 2003

61

ARCHBISHOP'S HOUSE,
WESTMINSTER, LONDON, SW1P 1QJ

13 January 2004

Dear NSPCC,

I had the good fortune to have a very happy childhood, being the youngest of five brothers to be followed years later by a much welcome sister.

One childhood memory is of my fifth birthday which was celebrated with my family, uncles and aunts and their families. I remember having my school cap and one of my uncles suggested I go round all my uncles and aunts with the cap and ask for a donation for the birthday boy!! I cannot remember how much I collected! It was not the money that was important but the real and abiding sense of family, security and love that we all felt at that picnic celebration. It is one of my earliest and happiest memories.

I hope that your book will evoke in your readers the sort of happy memories of which every childhood should be full – and raise plenty of money to help your work for vulnerable children everywhere.

With kind wishes,

Yours sincerely,

+Cormac Card. Murphy O'Connor

Archbishop of Westminster

G LBBON

64

One of my favourite childhood memories goes back to the time when I was very small, probably about three years of age.

At that time I was growing up in a northern suburb of Liverpool in a semi-detached house. Next door lived my grandfather and grandmother.

One of my greatest pleasures, as I recall, was to go in next door during the afternoon. There I would find my grandmother asleep on the sofa. Very gently, I would wake her up and say "Grandma, let's go to the zoo".

With infinite patience she would get up and come with me so that we were crouching down behind the back of the sofa looking across the room. The room then became the zoo. We would talk to each other of the giraffes and the lions, the snakes and the monkeys, the elephants and the hippopotamuses that we could see in our shared mind's eye. It was great fun.

Of course, as a child I had no idea how long these visits would last. Perhaps they lasted only a few moments. Perhaps they went on much longer into the afternoon. But I remember them vividly. To this day, I am grateful to my grandma for joining in my imaginings.

Isn't it wonderful the way that age need not separate the generations and how children and grandparents can enrich each other.

With every good wish,

Yours sincerely

✠Vincent Nichols
Archbishop of Birmingham

My hobby is football. Nearly every Saturday I play football for the cubs and my position on the pitch is full back and the goalkeeper is Gordon Willows.

In our first match we played Buckhorn Weston but we didn't have to work hard, because the size of the centre forward was about 3 ft nine inches and our forwards were attacking nearly all the time. After half time the opposing side were starting to pressurize us and one winger nearly scored. After a couple of minutes the whistle blew for full time and we went to change. We won 11.0.

NICKY AGE 10

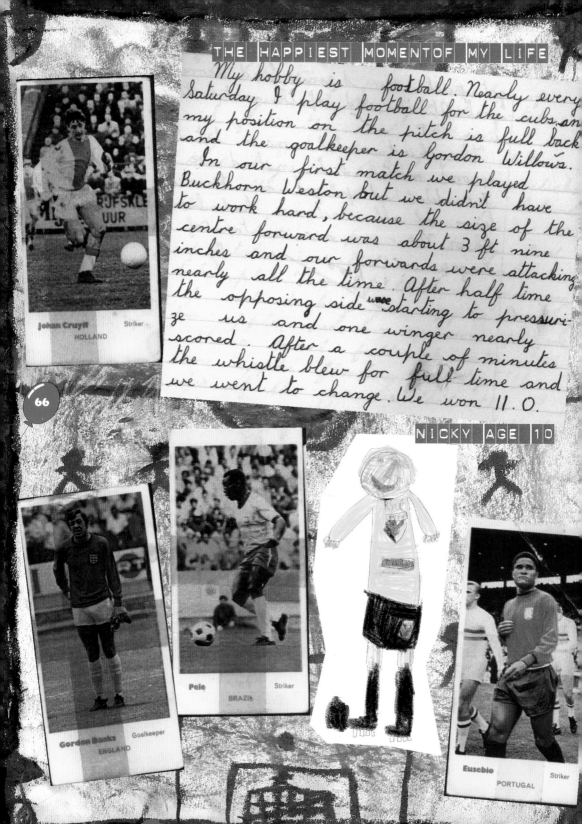

Johan Cruyff · Striker
HOLLAND

66

Gordon Banks · Goalkeeper
ENGLAND

Pele · Striker
BRAZIL

Eusebio · Striker
PORTUGAL

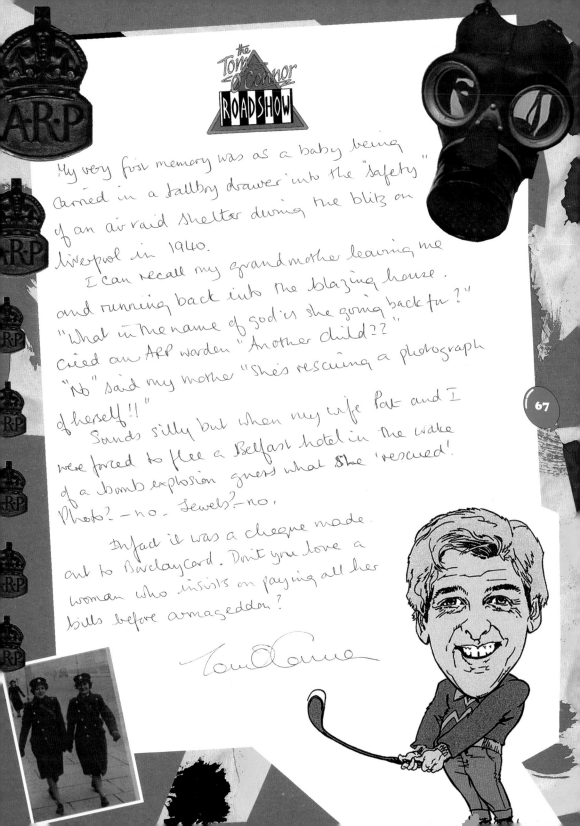

My very first memory was as a baby being carried in a tallboy drawer into the "safety" of an air raid shelter during the blitz on Liverpool in 1940.

I can recall my grandmother leaving me and running back into the blazing house. "What in the name of god is she going back for?" cried an ARP warden "Another child??" "No" said my mother "She's rescuing a photograph of herself!!"

Sounds silly but when my wife Pat and I were forced to flee a Belfast hotel in the wake of a bomb explosion guess what she 'rescued'. Photo? - no. Jewels? - no,

Infact it was a cheque made out to Barclaycard. Don't you love a woman who insists on paying all her bills before armageddon?

Tom O'Connor

12 January 2004

Dear Sir or Madam,

From the age of 5 and until the age of 7, I went to a Rudolf Steiner School. Rudolf Steiner was a very spiritual man and he said that school up to the age of 10 should be a beautiful, enjoyable and loving experience.

There were always beautiful colours around, painting, dancing and lots of music. It was a truly enjoyable time full of light and fun.

It was a bit of a shock when at the age of 7 I was sent to boarding school and found that I was behind in all the basic teaching. However I soon caught up, but I do believe that Steiner was right and that in time anyone can catch up. Nowadays it is targets, exams and pressure but no one can take away my beautiful and loving memories of my first school days.

Yours ever,

WILLIAM ROACHE, MBE.

CORONATION ST.

Best Wishes to all at NSPCC

William Roache

Dear NSPCC

You asked me for a childhood memory. Many of my strongest such memories are of my grandfather, one of the most powerful influences in my life.

William Foyle was a wonderful grandfather. He was kind, fun and witty, childlike and learned. He gave his grandchildren a love of books and mischief in equal measure, and encouraged us to help others and see good in all people. For all his considerable wealth he never lost his common touch or cockney accent.

As children we would wander round his bookshop, gather up an armful of books and stagger back to his office with them for him to confirm that we could have them, which he always did. Childhood was a paradise of unlimited books.

When we stayed with him at his wonderful old house, which we did for a week or so every school holiday, he would spend hours playing with us, croquet and bowls on fine days, cards in the evenings. He cheated outrageously but somehow we always finished up winning. He used to take us to the amusement park in Southend, the Kursaal. He would of course pay for us to go on any rides we wanted and always this would attract other children, for whom he would also pay. Sometimes we would have ten or more total strangers joining us, happily following this source of free rides and ice creams, a tubby, silver haired, genial latter-day Pied Piper.

There was a family ritual, very precious to us all: Every Friday, lunch at the Trocadero Restaurant in Shaftesbury Avenue for any of his large family who were in town. I remember the staff at the Troc: Mr Woods the head waiter, always ready to be the butt of Grandad's jokes, always falling for the electric shock handshake, the bread roll slipped into his pocket; and the impressive Sikh gentleman serving curries from a trolley, always delicious. I remember how the band always played "The Happy Wanderer", Grandad's favourite song, for us. I remember the pride I felt as a little boy to be associated with such a great and kind and lovable and loved man. And I remember, years later shortly after Grandad died, that we went back to the Troc to try to maintain the ritual; Mr Woods, still there, served us, with tears trickling down his face. We never went back as a family.

I visited Grandad for the last time when he was dying after suffering a stroke. He couldn't speak; he was sitting up in his big old four-poster bed, supported by Mr Quy, the gardener, who was sitting on the pillows holding him up so he wouldn't seem too incapable while the maid fed him. Mr Quy was crying, quietly but quite unashamedly. Two days later Grandad died. He was a wonderful eccentric, and I miss him still. He brought joy into many lives. He also introduced books to so many people through his lovely, organised-chaos, bookshop, in his time without question the finest in the world.

With all best wishes

Bill Samuel

Bill Samuel

AGENT FOR FOYLE'S 2<u>D</u> LIBRARY.

AGENT FOR FOYLE'S 2<u>D</u> LIBRARY

BRIAN SEWELL

14.i.2004

Dear Panjandrums of the NSPCC,

I hated most of my schoolmasters, none more than Mr. Callan, an English master whom I unreservedly detested.   I was in the third form, a short-trousered twelve, when the miserable year began.   English was a subject in which I was strong – very well read for my age and with an instinctive grasp of grammar – but Callan, nicknamed Nat for reasons now forgotten –though he introduced us to the sonnet and to Keats, pilloried me for my speech in almost every lesson.   God knows I had a tough enough time with other boys over the way I spoke, tougher by far than any gutteral German-Jewish boy, but to be mocked for it by my English master was incomprehensible.   It was Callan's custom to make me read aloud while he stood by my desk, half facing me, his head cocked on one side.   Every so often he stopped me and, turning to the class, picked on the pronunciation of a word.   "Sewell says appreciate sounding the <u>c</u> as though it were an <u>s</u>.   Who else does that?"   Not one boy, it seemed – or none was foolish enough to admit it – whereupon Callan, after accusing me of prissiness and affectation, asked "How then do you pronounce appreciation?"   And inevitably I was ridiculed for illogic in not sounding the <u>t</u> as a <u>t</u> instead of <u>sh</u>.

These bouts were always humiliating and I always lost.   The remedy was obvious – to learn to speak as other boys did – but I had little ear for the difference (and still do not, unless it is extreme) and no capacity for mimicry, though I knew and know when I am being mimicked.   Besides, there

was the problem of betrayal. I spoke as I spoke because it was the way my
immediate elders spoke at home, and to adopt a form of oral camouflage
because Callan was so bloody-minded did indeed seem a form of cowardly
betrayal. I could not do it. I did not want to do it. I began to skip
Callan's classes, spending the hour behind the fives courts or in the
lavatory when it was cold and wet, though, without a watch, this brought
other difficulties and air raids occasionally complicated matters. As I
could not altogether avoid Callan I had always to be ready with excuses for
absence and having done no prep, and was surprised when, as they grew more
and more improbable, he accepted them without question.

I sank from the top to the bottom of the class, but did not care - did
not care, that is, until my stepfather received an end of term report in
which Callan had written none of the conventions about trying harder,
reserved for failing pupils, only the brief note "Is a plausible liar."
I thought I had been implausible. I cannot recall the resolution of the
paradox.

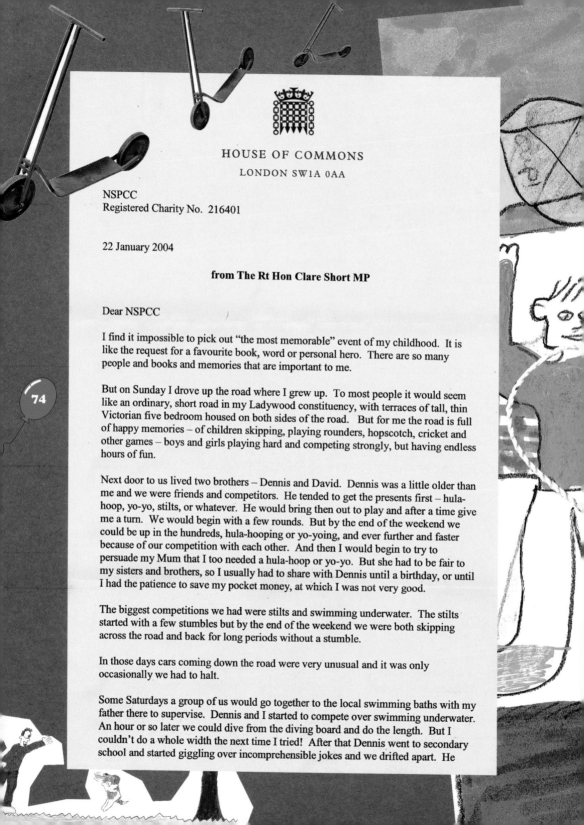

HOUSE OF COMMONS

LONDON SW1A 0AA

NSPCC
Registered Charity No. 216401

22 January 2004

from The Rt Hon Clare Short MP

Dear NSPCC

I find it impossible to pick out "the most memorable" event of my childhood. It is like the request for a favourite book, word or personal hero. There are so many people and books and memories that are important to me.

But on Sunday I drove up the road where I grew up. To most people it would seem like an ordinary, short road in my Ladywood constituency, with terraces of tall, thin Victorian five bedroom housed on both sides of the road. But for me the road is full of happy memories – of children skipping, playing rounders, hopscotch, cricket and other games – boys and girls playing hard and competing strongly, but having endless hours of fun.

Next door to us lived two brothers – Dennis and David. Dennis was a little older than me and we were friends and competitors. He tended to get the presents first – hula-hoop, yo-yo, stilts, or whatever. He would bring then out to play and after a time give me a turn. We would begin with a few rounds. But by the end of the weekend we could be up in the hundreds, hula-hooping or yo-yoing, and ever further and faster because of our competition with each other. And then I would begin to try to persuade my Mum that I too needed a hula-hoop or yo-yo. But she had to be fair to my sisters and brothers, so I usually had to share with Dennis until a birthday, or until I had the patience to save my pocket money, at which I was not very good.

The biggest competitions we had were stilts and swimming underwater. The stilts started with a few stumbles but by the end of the weekend we were both skipping across the road and back for long periods without a stumble.

In those days cars coming down the road were very unusual and it was only occasionally we had to halt.

Some Saturdays a group of us would go together to the local swimming baths with my father there to supervise. Dennis and I started to compete over swimming underwater. An hour or so later we could dive from the diving board and do the length. But I couldn't do a whole width the next time I tried! After that Dennis went to secondary school and started giggling over incomprehensible jokes and we drifted apart. He

joined the Sally army because he said he wanted to learn the trumpet. I do not know what became of him since.

Simple things: a street of playing children, very few cars, lots of happy memories. On top of that was the spice and achievement of my competition with Dennis. I hope he is well and happy now.

Best wishes

Clare Short

75

I spent several holidays with my Mother's sister Florence who was one of the original policewomen, then stationed at Croydon. Each morning I would set off by myself on a train to Westminster to discover London on foot – the only way. So started another of my obsessions, a love of the Metropolis which I now list as one of my principle hobbies. Keeping to Grandpa's dictum of always looking up, I roamed the streets of Westminster, the City, St. James's, Mayfair – all magical names to a country boy. Looking one day at the enormous nude statue of Achilles at Hyde Park Corner I heard a Londoner saying to a visitor, 'No, no, dear – Big Ben is a clock'. I spent hours in the British Museum, the Victoria and Albert Museum and the Maritime Museum, Westminster Abbey, St Paul's and the many City churches. Pop introduced me to the Sir John Soane Museum, which has remained my favourite refuge. He also took us to see the rehearsal of George VI's coronation, and I have never regretted not seeing the real thing. The bands and marching feet of the Guards were thrilling and during a temporary halt we were able to study, and even touch, Kent's magnificent fairy-take golden coach with its decoration by Cipriani.

Donald Sinden, *A Touch of the Memoirs* (Hodder & Stoughton, 1982). ISBN: 0340262354.

SIR JOHN SOANE'S
MUSEUM
Open Tuesday–Saturday
10 AM – 5 PM
(6–9 pm on the first Tuesday
of the month)

ADMISSION FREE

Groups must book in advance
(no groups on Saturdays)
TEL 020-7405-2107
Lecture tour on Saturday 2:30
(tickets £3 available from 2:00)

ACCESS BY APPOINTMENT TO THE LIBRARY AND
COLLECTIONS OF DRAWINGS & MANUSCRIPTS
TO BE ARRANGED BY TELEPHONE IN ADVANCE

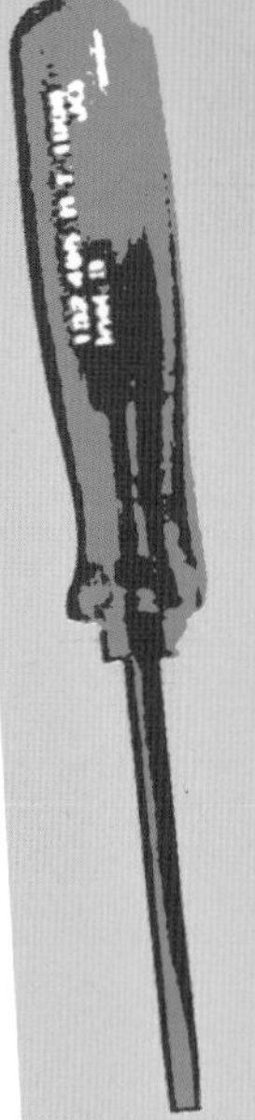

I will always remember my first experience of DIY, unintentional as it was!

I was about 8 yrs old and I had just learned how to do a handstand. Obviously I was very keen to demonstrate my new found skill and did so against the lounge wall..... in my wellington boots.... which were caked in mud......

Luckily mum was busy in the kitchen and Dad wasn't home from work yet, so I used a damp cloth on the stain (a little too vigourously it would seem) until I rubbed away the anaglypta wallpaper leaving a grubby hole 'I know, I'll paint over it!' I thought as I'd seen Dad do, year in year out to 'freshen' the room up. I knew where he kept the paints and soon I was splashing white paint over it ..... that would be white GLOSS paint over it.... After realising a hairdryer was not going to diminish the wet look I gave up and hid behind the piano until Dad got home. Heaven knows, we all suffered in the long run as he insisted on repainting the entire room, taking several days of huffing and puffing to do so. It has remained a great family joke ever since.

carol smillie

79

One of my happiest memories of childhood involves breaking the law. Nothing too serious, of course, and it was my mother who was in the driving seat – literally. She was disabled. She had been diagnosed with multiple sclerosis before I was born, but had been determined to go ahead with the pregnancy against all medical advice. By the time I could walk, she couldn't. Then in the late 1960s, when I was about seven, the government started issuing what it called Invalid Carriages or Invacars to disabled people. Built like a Reliant Robin, but without the styling, this sky blue three-wheeled chariot carried on the dashboard, next to the fire extinguisher, a stark warning notice: 'No passengers'. It was something to do with insurance and possibly also stability. This was a car built for one.

But it was also our only way of getting round together, so I would sit on the floor on a cushion, leaning against her folded-up wheelchair. I was out of sight because my presence was illegal. Perhaps that's why we laughed so much as we chugged along. The engine sounded like knives and forks put in a washing machine on fast spin. On one occasion we nearly got caught. There had been an accident and the police were redirecting the traffic. A constable, no doubt thinking that a disabled driver needed special instructions, bent forward to speak through the window as the Invacar approached, but my mother sped on by with a wave, knocking off his helmet. It was a close shave. And a hoot.

There was an attitude then – which sadly remains to this day – that children of disabled parents are somehow disadvantaged or even 'at risk'. While this may indeed be true in some cases, I hope my own wonderful childhood with a mother whose disability I never really noticed shows another side of the story.

Peter Stanford

The Happiest Moment of My Life

My happiest moment in my life was going on a plane for the last ever time before my dad died. I was going to America with my mum and my dad. My mum and dad knew that it was the last ever holiday. It was the best ever!

And I loved it!

My Hopes for the Future

I hope that in the future my mum finds someone nice to share her life with. I hope that he will help her to get through life.

I hope that my Dad is OK and that he is proud of me when he watches me.

By Sabrina Age 10

Dear NSPCC,

You asked me to share a special childhood memory with you and the one that springs to mind is the first time that I was ever taken to the theatre.

Firstly, I should add that I didn't actually know what a theatre was at the tender age of seven. I knew about television which I watched all the time, even though it was a tiny black and white flickering thing which my dad would thump occasionally when the signal went. But theatre? Never heard of it and didn't need to, living as I was in a tiny mining village in the Midlands where the local entertainment was the pub, the working man's club and the church, in that order.

So when the Sunday School organized a trip to a Pantomime, I was really excited when I was allowed to go. As my parents knew all the Sunday School teachers and all the other kids in the yard were going, it would have been cruel to leave me behind. So we all got on a very ancient coach with sticky seats which smelt faintly of cats, and off we went to the bustling metropolis of ... Stoke On Trent. 'Dick Whittington!' said the posters. I knew about him and his cat and his travels to London, I'd read all about it in the fairy tale book at school. But nothing prepared me for walking into what seemed like a palace, dramatically done out in red and gold, with rows of seats all facing a stage. And there was ice cream. It was already perfect and the play hadn't even begun!

And then when the music began and the actors came out on stage and began speaking, well, it was my first experience of Magic. Real magic, not in books or on TV, but real, in front of me, which smelled of baking lights and sweaty make up and melting ice cream and with hundreds of people gasping and laughing and booing and cheering all together, all feeling the same thing at the same time and I fell in love, just like that.

PUSS
IN
BOOTS.

London,
Printed and Sold by
J. T. WOOD, 278, Strand.

The best moment, and the one that is so vivid that I can still close my eyes now and conjure it up, was when Dick asked for a volunteer from the audience to come onto the stage. He had turned the villain into a dog, (can't remember why, must have been an important plot point), and wanted someone to come up and stroke him, to prove he had been tamed. I put my hand up, like everyone else, and Dick chose me! When I got onto the stage, my stomach heaved with nerves, my legs felt like jelly and for a moment, I thought I would pass out with excitement and terror. But then I took a breath and looked out at the audience, felt the boards beneath my feet, the spotlights on my face, and relaxed. I think I smiled, because I felt as if I'd just come home.

MEERA SYAL

28th November 2003

To all at the NSPCC

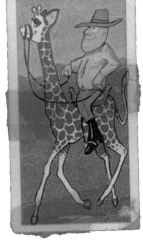

A childhood memory ...

My passion for fishing started as a very young child and some of my fondest childhood memories are being with my Grandad, Stanley Charles Tarrant, who was the first person to instil a love of the countryside in me and, in particular, teach me how to fish – both of which have remained a great passion in my life.

He used to go for the most amazingly long walks and I remember following him for mile after mile across the wild, open country of the Berkshire downs, with my little legs whirring along trying desperately to keep up with his great six-foot strides.

His idea of 'a good walk' was about 30 miles ! He lived in Reading and if he fancied a day's fishing at, say, Newbury on the River Kennet, about 15 or 16 miles away, he'd get up before sunrise and walk there. And if dad and I couldn't invent some perfectly reasonable excuse like a sudden recurrence of anthrax or a broken leg, we'd have to go too.

Grandad's extraordinary physical stamina was presumably a great help to him when he suddenly decided to get married again at the age of 85 !

He was always my best friend as a little boy and when he finally died at the age of 96, it was one of the saddest days of my life.

CHRIS TARRANT

12 January 2004

Dear NSPCC

I've been asked to give a memory from my childhood to include in the book *Once Upon A Time*, so here is a short affectionate tribute to a teacher who influenced me enormously.

"Ilkley All Saints Junior School was a Victorian building, one of those classic northern schools made of stone that had been blackened by a century of soot and now usually brightened up with turquoise door, which don't fool anybody. My favourite teacher of all time, Mr Rhodes, taught me in my second year there. Harry Rhodes was well spoken and jolly. It seemed that he was always smiling, always enthusiastic and always – most importantly – encouraging. Where other teachers would be of the 'Sit down and shut up' school of education, Harry Rhodes was the 'Get up and show me' type. If you showed the slightest aptitude for anything, he fanned the flame. It's down to him, as much as anyone, that I became a gardener.

Mr Rhodes – six feet, with a Roman nose on which perched a pair of rimless glasses – was a keen gardener. Cacti were his speciality. He would always give you a few handy hints on their cultivation: "Not too much water, drier in winter than in summer. Try it on a windowsill, Alan; it likes good light." He was the only teacher who occasionally called boys by their Christian names – he marked himself out as being all the more human because of his friendliness. Not that he was a pushover. Oh, no. He could maintain discipline with practised ease, and could achieve silence by the raising of an eyebrow.

Good teachers somehow manage to rise above the low pay, the ridiculous demands on their time and those disruptive kids who just don't seem to want to learn. They are at the other end of the spectrum from the teacher who bumped into me on Ilkley car park recently.
    'Titchmarsh!' she said, as though she couldn't believe her eyes.
    'Yes?'
    'Well!' she said, accusingly. 'We never thought you'd amount to much!'
    I felt as though I'd disappointed her."

Yours sincerely

from Alan Titchmarsh

My Childhood Memory

The Year was 1940 - the second world war was with us - I was fourteen years old. I went swimming with friends, unfortunately in a stagnant 'open air' pool, and caught Diphtheria. I was in hospital for three or four weeks, no visitors allowed and occasionally everyone in the ward was moved into the corridor as bombs were dropping nearby.

My favourite Dr. Ellison kept us all cheerful with his little 'ditties.' Here's one:-

Ellison is a noble man
He's just designed a new bed-pan,
You sit upon a rim of steel,
And that is really all you feel!

It was a fairly traumatic time but I survived the disease and the war so I consider myself very fortunate and am happy to contribute my story to your book *Once Upon A Time*.

Yours sincerely,

June Whitfield

June Whitfield, CBE

The
NORMAN WISDOM —
Official Fan Club

I was born in very sorry circumstances. Both my parents were very sorry!

I know that's an old Music Hall joke, but there's a ring of truth in it. Well, according to my Dad anyway!

I had a very tough childhood and my Father just didn't want to know me. He was very cruel to me, and I ended up sleeping rough. But I was determined to get on and I worked hard to achieve something in life, but it was joining the army that gave me the first step on the ladder. I had mates, a bed, food, travel, sport....and eventually showbiz!

If I look back on my life, I can't believe all the things I've done, the people I've met, the places I've been to....I really have been a Lucky Little Devil, and I wouldn't change it for the world.

Sir Norman Wisdom. O.B.E.

Sir Norman Wisdom, O.B.E.

The Maltings - Brewery Road
Hoddesdon, Herts. EN11 8HF

If I owe my literacy to anybody, apart from the sainted Michael and Rose, I owe it to Auntie May. Throughout my childhood and early adolescence, she kept me supplied with books, comics and magazines, that opened a new, different and wider world for a boy living in a parochial, narrow-minded town in the south-west of Ireland.

Her parcels would arrive every Friday without fail: Beano, Dandy, Wizard and Champion, Film and Radio Fun, and, later on, the miracle of shiny colour that was the Eagle. Every couple of weeks, a new book: progressing from *Dr Doolittle* to *Wind in the Willows*, on to *Just William* and *Billy Bunter*, to *Bulldog Drummond* and *The Thirty-Nine Steps*, my dear Auntie May inculcated in me a love of books and reading that has never left me, and has given me a breadth of vocabulary and general knowledge that I could never have otherwise reached.

Summer holidays in Irish schools were always three months long, with almost a month at Christmas and a couple of weeks at Easter. Often my mother and I would pop on the train up to the Big City, leaving the tireless, dutiful Michael to labour alone among the hams, jams and other comestibles of Limerick's finest victualler.

I loved these visits. Who wouldn't? For six years, until, against all expectations, my brother Brian turned up, I had the individual attention and affection of a granny, three maiden aunts and a mother . . .

What a life for a little chap - more comics, magazines and books than even Mr Voracious could read. And the pictures, at least once a week. Afterwards it was Cafolla's Caf, for a Knickerbocker Glory, a huge ice cream soda with every known variety of tinned fruit and syrup, topped with cream, and eaten with a long spoon. Oh, and it had jelly in it, as well.

Terry Wogan, *Is it me?* (BBC Worldwide Ltd, 2001). ISBN: 0563534222

"I believe we all have a certain time in our lives that we're good at. I wasn't good at being a child."

"They were horrible. All sisters are horrible. Well, mine were. Very bossy, and they treated me like a nuisance. They were very proficient at giving 'young Victoria' a good quashing, telling-off and bossing-about."

"... I was cruelly sat on, sat on and tormented for many years, and made to eat putty."

Neil Brandwood, *Victoria Wood ... The Biography* (Virgin Books, 2002) ISBN: 0753508613.

Dear NSPCC

We were standing on the fire escape desperate to look through the telescope. It was the fifties, I can't remember which year, but the Russians had just launched the first doggie cosmonaut and according to the local Brighton rag we would be able to see the space capsule fly over.

What could be going on in the head of Superdogski? Was it wearing a space suit complete with red underpants and a cape? How would it be feted on its return, gold plate bones, a silver dog bowl, Winalotski for life? Would it be given the freedom of dog city? It might even be granted an audience with The King, Elvis Presley. A dog tour must surely be on the cards with gold lamp-posts and ermin jewel-studded lead and collar. We would never know, nobody dashed my dreams, nobody explained the principles of communism, no bones, no special favours, no life . . .

Anthony Worrall–Thompson